The Art of Home Baking

The Art of Home Baking

100 Years of Baking Memories

EBURY
PRESS

OPINEL
INOX

Cook's Notes

Unless stated otherwise:

- All spoon measures are level.
- All eggs are medium.
- Stork® block should be used at room temperature.
- Beating of ingredients may be done with a wooden spoon or in a food mixer.
- Decrease the given Centigrade temperature by 20 degrees if using a fan oven.

Note: Gluten-free and vegan recipes are indicated with the symbols **Gf** and **V**.

Opposite Gluten-free Raspberry and Coconut Slice (see page 100).

Contents

Foreword by Ruby Bhogal 9

Introduction 11

Timeline 12

1 Bread, Scones and Muffins 15

2 Large Cakes 51

3 Small Cakes and Traybakes 83

4 Biscuits and Cookies 105

5 Tarts and Pies 127

6 Icings 153

7 Desserts 163

8 Occasion Bakes 187

Appendix 209

Index 222

Opposite Caramel Fingers
(see page 110).

COOKERY NOTES No. 53

Recipes approved by the Ministry of Food

MAY, 1944

Foreword by Ruby Bhogal

Happiness. Ask anyone about baking and I guarantee you it stems back to happiness. Happiness for you, your soul, those around you and, of course, everyone's tummy. Whether it's cake that takes your fancy, or bread that you devour the minute it is put in front of you, baking truly is a gift that provides a great foundation for building relationships, for entertaining, for showing appreciation of those around you, for celebrating your nearest and dearest, and for unfailingly spreading happiness among those who eat the bakes one delicious crumb at a time.

To say I owe a lot to baking is a ridiculous understatement. It's been an incredible creative outlet, and it has brought so much joy to me and those around me. It sounds dramatic, but it has quite literally changed my life (and waistline). When I got into baking, I didn't expect it to take me off on a different route in life, but am I mad at it for the change? Not in the slightest. No matter what your age or circumstances, baking has an appeal that is irresistible. Is it as sexy as cooking? Probably not. But is it as enticing? Even more so.

Baking, just like Stork®, is timeless and simple. I love how it evokes memories, how the smell of a freshly baked cake can bring on a wave of nostalgia, and how the taste can slap a silly grin across most faces. Stork® has been encouraging and helping people do just that for the past 100 years, its delicious versatility lending itself to everything from a classic Victoria sponge to modern vegan bakes. To my mind, Stork® is a key ingredient in ensuring that baking is simple and successful.

Enjoy this book. Devour and savour every last page. Drool over the possibilities. Learn from it. Delight in it. Create new memories. Fall in love with the power of baking. And from it, I truly hope you keep yourself and those around you forever happy.

Celebrating 100 Years of Baking with Stork®

Happy birthday, Stork®! We're proud to have been the secret ingredient of British bakers for a century. To celebrate our 100th year, we've brought together 100 of our favourite bakes in a new edition of *The Art of Home Baking*.

We still believe nothing beats home baking, and the joyful, tasty memories it creates. Who doesn't remember their Grandma's afternoon tea, childhood birthday cakes and the bakes that marked graduation, anniversaries or simply a much-needed catch-up over a cuppa? We're delighted to help you continue serving up some classic favourites, along with a selection of new recipes created specially in celebration of our centenary.

We hope this book helps and inspires you to bake more happy memories for the next 100 years.

Opposite Lemon Meringue Pie (see page 128).

Timeline

1920 Stork® was introduced as a tasty alternative to butter. It was promoted by a series of press advertisements, reminding consumers of Stork®'s energy-giving qualities.

1939–45 When it became clear that Britain was going to war, rationing quickly came into force, and the Stork® Cookery Service was set up to help provide ingenious recipe ideas in those challenging times. The service published *The Stork Wartime Cookbook*, which featured recipes such as meatless pies, eggless cakes and sugarless desserts, all developed to help households economise in times of shortage. The cookbook even offered advice on what to do if an air-raid warning interrupted cooking. In the spirit of pulling together in times of need, it was decided by manufacturers to halt the distribution of branded margarine during the war, thereby maximising the total production output.

1954 Stork®, in its traditional packaging, returned to the shelves, and the Cookery Service continued printing a series of helpful booklets, with detailed recipes for all occasions. It was at this time that *The Art of Home Cooking* was first published, and it proved hugely popular, selling tens of thousands of copies. In fact, it became a staple recipe book for households and is still used by many to this day.

1956 After the war, a thirst for knowledge and ideas led to the creation of the Stork® Wives Club. Members could write to Stork®'s expert chefs, who would answer any culinary questions, and also attend cooking demonstrations that were held up and down the country. This was a vital service to those who had grown up without staple ingredients, and to households who were forced to create meals with limited supplies. At the peak of the club's popularity, it had over a quarter of a million members, but was eventually disbanded in 1970.

1970s–80s Throughout these decades, several famous faces, including Bruce Forsyth and Leslie Crowther, featured in a series of Stork® television campaigns, where the public participated in blind taste tests to identify Stork® against other brands.

2002 The now-familiar yellow Stork® tubs were launched, with clear measuring guides and tips for easy family baking recipes.

Today Stork® is best known by Britain's home bakers as the secret ingredient for creating light and fluffy cakes. Times and tastes may have changed since the days of wartime rationing, but the British public's love of Stork® has remained as great as ever.

1
Bread, Scones and Muffins

Basic White Bread

There's nothing quite as wonderful as the smell of homemade bread, and this recipe (apart from proving time) takes only 20 minutes to put together, so why not make a loaf for all the family to enjoy?

MAKES 1 LARGE LOAF

500g (1lb 2oz) strong white bread flour, plus extra for dusting (optional)

1 x 7g sachet easy-blend yeast

1½ tsp salt

1 tsp sugar

130ml (4¼fl oz) boiling water

25g (1oz) Stork® block

200ml (7fl oz) milk

Vegetable oil, for greasing

1. Place the flour, yeast, salt and sugar in a bowl and stir together.
2. Measure the boiling water in a jug. Add the Stork® and stir until melted, then add the milk. The liquid should now be hand hot.
3. Add the liquid to the flour and stir well, until the mixture comes together.
4. Turn onto a lightly floured work surface and knead for 10 minutes by hand, or 5 minutes in an electric mixer fitted with a dough hook.
5. When the dough is smooth and elastic, return it to the bowl, cover with oiled clingfilm and leave in a warm place for 45–60 minutes, until doubled in size.
6. Lightly oil a 900g (2lb) loaf tin. Punch back the dough to knock out the air, then turn it onto the work surface and shape into a rectangle. Roll it up and drop it into the prepared tin. Place inside a plastic bag, making sure the bag doesn't touch the top of the dough, and leave to rise again until doubled in size.
7. Preheat the oven to 220°C/425°F/Gas Mark 7.
8. Dust the dough with flour if you like, then use a very sharp knife to make a slash along the length of it.
9. Bake in the centre of the oven for 15 minutes, then lower the temperature to 200°C/400°F/Gas Mark 6 and bake for a further 15–20 minutes, until golden brown and sounding hollow when tapped on the bottom. Turn onto a wire rack and leave to cool completely.

First produced in the late 1950s, this booklet proved so popular that it was reissued several times. The emphasis was on sandwich fillings that were imaginative yet nutritionally sound.

Sandwich Making
the Stork way!

Traditional Brown Bread

Guests will be highly impressed when you serve homemade bread with a bowl of soup, some pâté or cheese and chutney. This quick and easy recipe can be made into loaves or individual rolls.

MAKES 2 X 500G (1LB) LOAVES OR 8–10 ROLLS

Vegetable oil, for greasing

750g (1½lb) granary flour or plain wholemeal flour, plus extra for dusting

2 tsp salt

25g (1oz) Stork® block

1 x 7g sachet easy-blend yeast

450ml (15fl oz) warm water

1. Oil 2 x 500g (1lb) loaf tins, or a large baking sheet.
2. Mix the flour and salt in a bowl, rub in the Stork®, then stir in the yeast. Add the water and mix to form a dough.
3. Turn onto a lightly floured work surface and knead for 10 minutes by hand, or 5 minutes in an electric mixer fitted with a dough hook.
4. When the dough is smooth and elastic, divide and shape it as required, then place in the prepared tins or on the baking sheet. Cover with oiled clingfilm and leave in a warm place until doubled in size.
5. Preheat the oven to 230°C/450°F/Gas Mark 8.
6. Bake the loaves for about 25 minutes (or 35 minutes for a 1kg/2lb loaf), until they sound hollow when tapped on the bottom. Bake the rolls for about 15 minutes.
7. Turn onto a wire rack and leave to cool completely.

Warm rolls fresh from the oven appeal to everyone, hence this booklet, which encouraged home cooks to bake bread in all its forms.

GREAT
BRITISH BAKING

Cheesy Walnut Rolls

Crusty bread rolls swirled with cheese and walnuts are irresistible. You will want to enjoy these warm from the oven, or packed for a picnic or delicious lunchbox.

MAKES 9

50g (2oz) Stork® spread, plus extra for brushing

Vegetable oil, for greasing

350g (12oz) strong white flour, sifted, plus extra for dusting

10g (4oz) plain wholemeal flour

1 tsp salt

1 x 7g sachet easy-blend yeast

300ml (10fl oz) warm milk or half warm water, half milk

Milk, to glaze

FOR THE FILLING

25g (1oz) Stork® spread, melted

100g (4oz) Cheddar cheese, grated

25g (1oz) walnuts, finely chopped

1. Brush an 18–20cm (7–8 inch) square tin with melted Stork®. Oil a large bowl.
2. Place the flours and salt in a clean large bowl. Rub in the Stork® until the mixture resembles fine breadcrumbs.
3. Add the yeast and stir well, then pour in the liquid and stir until a soft dough forms (you might need to add a little extra warm water).
4. Turn onto a lightly floured work surface and knead well until smooth (about 10 minutes by hand, or 5 minutes in an electric mixer fitted with a dough hook).
5. Shape the dough into a ball and place it in the oiled bowl. Cover with oiled clingfilm and leave in a warm place until doubled in size (about 45–60 minutes).
6. Turn the dough onto the work surface, punch firmly to knock out the air, then knead until smooth and firm.
7. Roll into a rectangle about 30 x 23cm (12 x 9 inches).
8. Brush with the melted Stork® and sprinkle with the cheese and walnuts. Roll up from the longest side, and dampen the edge to seal.
9. Cut into 9 slices and place them in the prepared tin, cut side uppermost. Brush with milk, cover with oiled clingfilm and leave to rise in a warm place for about 30 minutes.
10. Preheat the oven to 200°C/400°F/Gas Mark 6. Bake the rolls for about 30–45 minutes, until risen and golden. Serve with soup or salad.

From simple tea parties to elaborate dinners, the Stork® Cookery Service was full of new ideas for every occasion.

Plain and Fancy
FROM THE
STORK COOKERY SERVICE

Garlic and Herb Tear-and-Share Bread

If you have a crowd of friends around for supper, place this bread in the centre of the table, serve with cold meats and cheeses, and wait for the compliments. It's fun and easy to make too.

SERVES 8

Vegetable oil, for greasing

500g (1lb 2oz) strong white bread flour, plus extra for dusting

1½ tsp easy-blend yeast

1½ tsp salt

1 tsp sugar

2 tsp mixed dried herbs

135ml (4½fl oz) boiling water

25g (1oz) Stork® spread

200ml (7fl oz) milk

FOR THE TOPPING

75g (3oz) Stork® spread

2 garlic cloves, crushed

2 tbsp finely chopped parsley

1 tsp chopped oregano, fresh or dried

1. Lightly oil a 20cm (8 inch) round cake tin.
2. Place the flour, yeast, salt, sugar and herbs in a bowl and stir together. Measure the boiling water into a measuring jug, add the Stork® and stir until melted. Add the milk, then pour this liquid into the flour mixture and mix well until a dough forms.
3. Turn the dough onto a lightly floured work surface and knead until smooth and elastic (10 minutes by hand, or 5 minutes in an electric mixer fitted with a dough hook).
4. Return the dough to the bowl, cover with oiled clingfilm and set aside in a warm place until doubled in size (45–60 minutes).
5. To make the topping, melt the Stork® in a pan, add the garlic and herbs, then set aside to cool a little.
6. Punch the risen dough to knock out the air, then turn it onto a lightly floured work surface. Cut it into 8 equal pieces and roll each one into a ball. Dip the top of each ball in the garlic and herb mixture, then arrange in the prepared tin.
7. Cover loosely with oiled clingfilm and set aside again in a warm place until doubled in size.
8. Preheat the oven to 220°C/425°F/Gas Mark 7.
9. Bake the bread for 15 minutes, then lower the temperature to 200°C/400°F/Gas Mark 6 and bake for a further 15–20 minutes, until golden brown. Allow to cool for 15 minutes and serve hot or cold.

Cranberry and Mixed Seed Bloomer

Packed with fruit and nuts, this is a great loaf to serve for breakfast, but also ideal alongside a cheese board, and good for sandwiches too.

MAKES 1 LARGE LOAF

Vegetable oil, for greasing
500g (1lb 2oz) wholemeal flour with mixed grains
1 tsp salt
1½ tsp easy-blend yeast
25g (1oz) Stork® block
300ml (10fl oz) milk
1 tbsp light brown sugar
100g (4oz) dried cranberries
1 tbsp mixed seeds
1 tbsp oats

1. Lightly oil a baking tray.
2. Place the flour, salt and yeast in a bowl, add the Stork® and rub in until the mixture resembles breadcrumbs.
3. Add the milk and sugar and mix to form a soft dough. Turn the dough onto a work surface and knead until smooth and elastic (10 minutes by hand, or 5 minutes in an electric mixer fitted with a dough hook).
4. Add the cranberries and seeds and knead them into the dough until evenly distributed.
5. Shape the dough into an oval bloomer and place on the prepared baking tray. Cover with oiled clingfilm and leave in a warm place until doubled in size.
6. Preheat the oven to 220°C/425°F/Gas Mark 7.
7. Sprinkle the risen dough with the oats, then make a lengthways slash in the top. Bake for 15 minutes, then reduce the heat to 180°C/350°F/Gas Mark 4 and bake for another 15 minutes, covering the dough with non-stick baking paper if it gets a little too brown.
8. Cool on a wire rack, then serve sliced with cheese.

To help the war effort, only non-branded spread was produced during the war years. It was a cause of celebration when Stork® eventually returned to the shelves.

Same rich Vitamin food...
at the same price!

Fruity Irish Soda Bread

Originally from Teatime with Stork*, produced by the Stork® Cookery Service in the 1950s, this recipe is the quickest, easiest bread to make – moist, a little crumbly and packed with flavour. It's so good, you'll be tempted to make it every week.*

MAKES 1 LOAF

50–75g (2–3oz) Stork® spread, plus extra for brushing

450g (1 lb) plain flour, plus extra for dusting

1 tsp salt

1 rounded tsp each bicarbonate of soda and cream of tartar, or 4 rounded tsp baking powder

2 rounded tbsp sugar

100g (4oz) dried fruit, e.g. sultanas, currants, dates or prunes

50g (2oz) chopped peel

375ml (13fl oz) sour milk

1. Preheat the oven to 200°C/400°F/Gas Mark 6. Brush an 18cm (7 inch) cake tin with melted Stork®.
2. Sift the flour, salt and raising agent(s) into a bowl. Rub in the Stork® until the mixture resembles breadcrumbs, then stir in the sugar, fruit and peel.
3. Make a well in the centre of the flour mixture, pour in the sour milk and mix with a knife to form a soft dough.
4. Turn the dough onto a well-floured work surface, flour your hands and knead the dough until smooth (10 minutes by hand, or 5 minutes in an electric mixer fitted with a dough hook).
5. Form into an 18cm (7 inch) circle, make a cross in the top with a knife, then place in the prepared tin. Bake for 1 hour, then lower the temperature to 180°C/350°F/Gas Mark 4 and bake for a further 30 minutes.
6. Turn onto a wire rack to cool. Serve thinly sliced and spread with Stork®.

Banana Loaf

Here's the perfect recipe for using up those overripe bananas in the fruit bowl. It's so simple and easy to make, and there's only one mixing bowl to wash up.

SERVES 12

75g (3oz) Stork® spread, plus extra for brushing
225g (8oz) brown sugar
3 ripe bananas, mashed
1 egg
600ml (1 pint) milk
¼ tsp ground mixed spice
450g (1lb) plain flour
2 tsp bicarbonate of soda

1. Preheat the oven to 180°C/350°F/Gas Mark 4. Brush a 900g (2lb) loaf tin with melted Stork®.
2. Cream the Stork® in a bowl, add the sugar and bananas, and mix thoroughly.
3. Beat in the egg and milk.
4. Sift the dry ingredients together, then quickly fold them into the banana mixture, adding a little more milk, if necessary, to make a soft dropping consistency.
5. Pour the batter into the prepared tin and bake for 1–1½ hours, until golden brown, just firm to the touch and a skewer inserted in the centre comes out clean.
6. Turn the loaf onto a wire rack to cool. Slice when cold and spread with Stork® before serving.

Note: This bread keeps well if wrapped in greaseproof paper and stored in an airtight container. If preferred, it can be baked in two 450g (1lb) loaf tins placed side by side for 45 minutes.

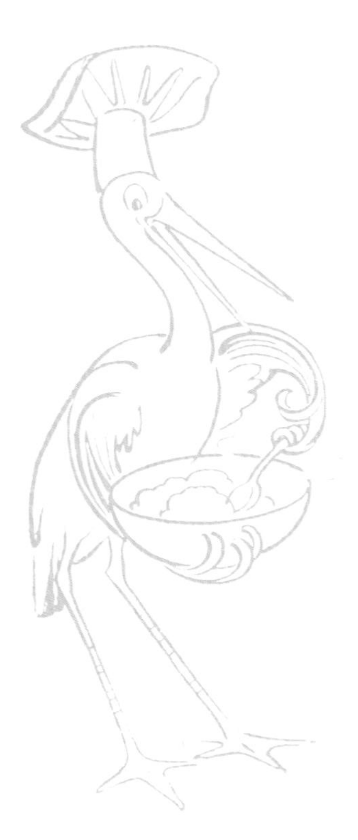

Cinnamon and Raisin Chelsea Buns

These are the perfect weekend bake – fun to make and especially good when still slightly warm from the oven – a true family treat.

MAKES 8

15g (½oz) Stork® spread, plus extra for brushing

225g (8oz) strong white flour, plus extra for dusting

½ tsp salt

1 x 7g sachet easy-blend dried yeast

1 egg, beaten

100ml (3½fl oz) warm milk

FOR THE FILLING

25g (1oz) Stork® spread, melted

40g (1½oz) soft brown sugar

75g (3oz) raisins

1 tsp ground cinnamon

FOR THE GLACÉ ICING

50g (2oz) icing sugar, sifted

Few drops of orange juice

1. Brush a 20cm (8 inch) square or round cake tin with melted Stork®.
2. Place the flour and salt in a bowl, rub in the Stork® until the mixture resembles breadcrumbs, then stir in the yeast. Add the egg and milk and mix to form a dough.
3. Turn onto a lightly floured work surface and knead well for 10 minutes by hand, or 5 minutes in an electric mixer fitted with a dough hook.
4. Roll the dough into a 30 x 22cm (12 x 9 inch) rectangle. Brush the melted Stork® over it and sprinkle with the other filling ingredients. Roll up lengthways like a Swiss roll and cut into 8 equal pieces.
5. Lay the slices cut side up in the prepared cake tin. Cover and leave to rise in a warm place for 15–20 minutes, until almost doubled in size.
6. Meanwhile, preheat the oven to 190°C/375°F/Gas Mark 5 and combine the icing ingredients in a bowl.
7. Uncover the buns and bake for 25–30 minutes. Drizzle with the icing and serve warm or cold.

VARIATION

Omit the cinnamon, reduce the raisins to 25g (1oz) and add 50g (2oz) chopped marzipan.

Home baking has always been a popular activity, but in the pre-war years it was considered an essential skill. Stork® produced many leaflets to help keen home bakers.

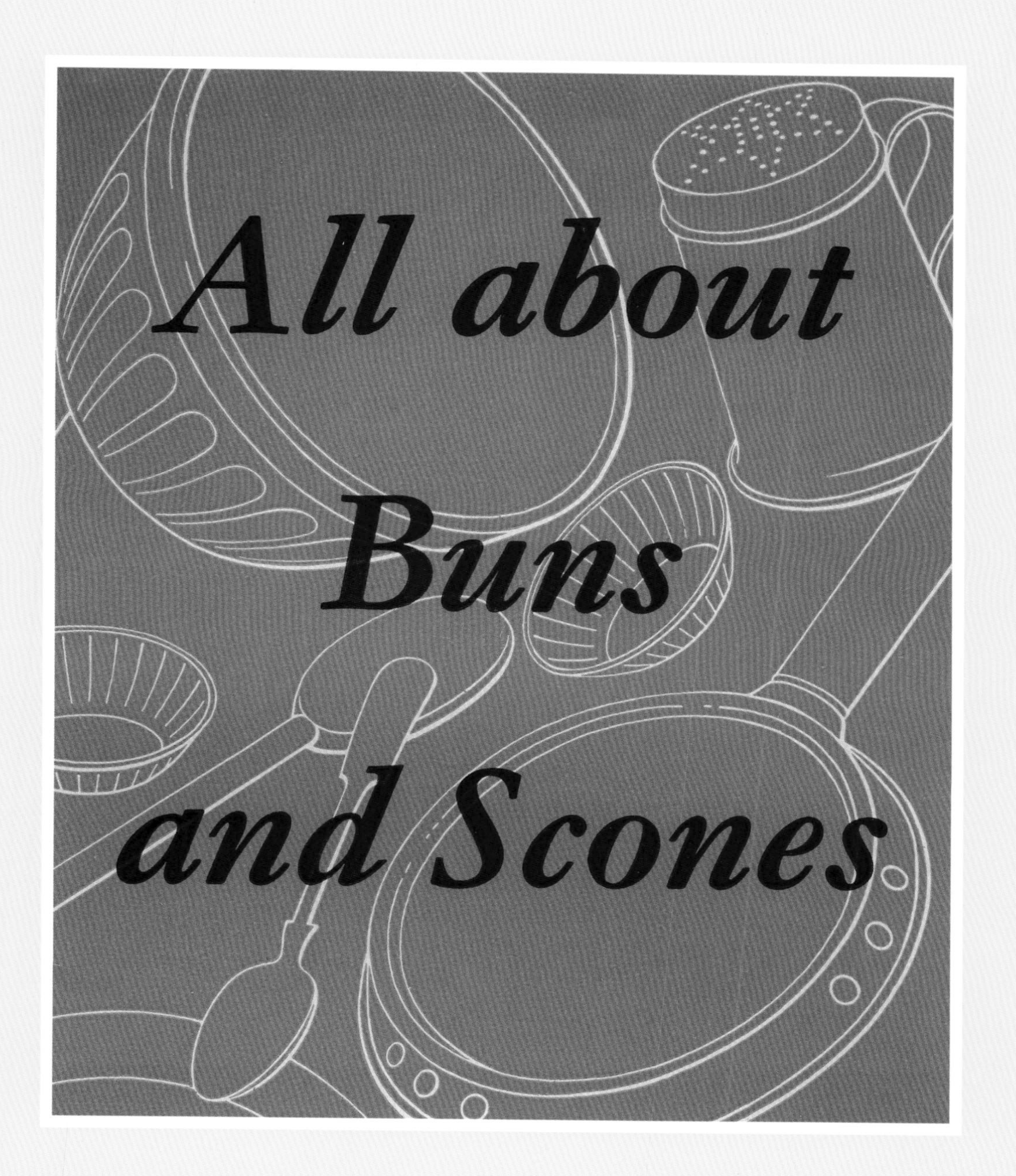

All about Buns and Scones

Baked S'mores Doughnuts

Coated with chocolate and sandwiched with toasted marshmallows, these doughnuts are a wonderful indulgence, and much easier to make than the yeasted, deep-fried versions.

MAKES 12

110g (4¼oz) Stork® spread, plus extra for brushing

100g (4oz) granulated sugar

70g (2¾oz) dark brown sugar

2 eggs

1 tsp baking powder

¼ tsp bicarbonate of soda

2 tsp ground cinnamon

½ tsp salt

1 tsp vanilla extract

300g (11 oz) plain flour

225ml (7½fl oz) milk

TO ASSEMBLE

14 marshmallows, cut in half

200g (7oz) milk chocolate, melted

50g (2oz) digestive biscuits, crushed (optional)

1. Preheat the oven to 220°C/425°F/Gas Mark 6. Brush two 6-hole doughnut trays with melted Stork®.
2. Cream the Stork® and sugars in a bowl until pale and fluffy. Beat in the eggs one at a time. Stir in the baking powder, bicarbonate, cinnamon, salt and vanilla. Finally, add one-third of the flour, followed by half the milk, repeating until all the flour and milk are used up.
3. Spoon the batter into a piping bag, snip off the end and pipe the mixture into the prepared trays.
4. Bake the doughnuts for 10 minutes. Allow to cool in the trays for 5 minutes, then turn them onto a wire rack to cool completely.
5. When cold, preheat the grill. Slice the doughnuts in half and arrange the bottom halves, cut side up, in a circle on a baking sheet. Top with the marshmallow halves, then place under the grill for 2–3 minutes, until melted and slightly toasted.
6. Whilst the marshmallows are toasting, dip the top halves of the doughnuts into the melted chocolate. Sit these 'lids' on top of the toasted halves and sprinkle with the crushed digestives, if using.

Traditional Scones

Friends coming round? Why not rustle up a batch of homemade scones to serve fresh from the oven and topped with cream and jam? This recipe has been delighting people since 1965, when it featured in the Plain and Fancy *leaflets produced by the Stork® Cookery Service.*

MAKES 10 x 6CM (2½ INCH) SCONES OR 16 x 4CM (1½ INCH) SCONES

50g (2oz) Stork® spread, plus extra for brushing

225g (8oz) self-raising flour, sifted with 1 tsp baking powder

25g (1oz) caster sugar

7 tbsp fresh or sour milk, plus extra fresh milk to glaze

1. Preheat the oven to 220°C/425°F/Gas Mark 7. Brush a baking sheet with melted Stork®.
2. **All-in-one method**: Place all the ingredients in a bowl and mix with a wooden spoon to form a soft dough.
   Rubbing-in method: Cut the Stork® into pieces and rub into the flour with your fingertips until the mixture resembles breadcrumbs. Add the sugar and milk and mix with a knife to form a soft dough.
3. Turn the dough onto a lightly floured surface and knead gently until smooth. Roll out to a thickness of 1cm (½ inch).
4. Using a plain 6cm (2½ inch) floured cutter, stamp out 10 circles, or use a plain 4cm (1½ inch) floured cutter and stamp out 16 circles. You will need to reroll the trimmings to get the required number.
5. Place the circles on the prepared baking sheet, brush the tops with extra milk and bake for 12–15 minutes, until risen and golden brown.
6. Serve either hot or cold, cut open and spread with Stork®.

   Note: Scones freeze well if packed in rigid plastic boxes or arranged in rows in freezer bags.

VARIATIONS

Cheese scones: Omit the sugar from the basic scone ingredients and add 100g (4oz) finely grated cheese, 1 teaspoon dry mustard, ¼ teaspoon salt and a pinch of cayenne pepper.

Fruit scones: Add 50–75g (2–3oz) dried fruit, e.g. currants, sultanas, chopped dates.

Wholemeal scones: Omit the sugar and use half self-raising white flour and half self-raising wholemeal flour. A little extra liquid will probably be needed too.

Honey Scones

A little twist on tradition, these scones have the delicate flavour of honey and are wonderful simply spread with Stork® and a touch more honey. The recipe first featured in leaflets produced by the Stork® Cookery Service during the 1940s.

MAKES 10–12

50g (2oz) Stork® spread, plus extra for brushing

225g (8oz) self-raising flour, plus extra for dusting

½ tsp mixed spice

2 rounded tsp caster sugar

2 tbsp clear honey, plus extra for brushing

6 tbsp milk

1. Preheat the oven to 220°C/425°F/Gas Mark 7. Brush a baking sheet with melted Stork®.
2. Sift the flour and mixed spice into a bowl. Stir in the sugar, then rub in the Stork® until the mixture resembles fine breadcrumbs.
3. Add the honey and milk and mix lightly with a knife to form a soft dough.
4. Turn onto a lightly floured work surface and roll out to a thickness of 2cm (¾ inch). Using a 5cm (2 inch) fluted cutter, stamp out 10–12 circles, rerolling the trimmings as necessary.
5. Place the circles on the prepared sheet and bake for 12–15 minutes.
6. Brush the scones with a little warmed honey, then cool on a wire rack.
7. Serve hot or cold, cut in half and spread with Stork® and honey.

Lemon and Raspberry Scones

Mini scones look so cute as part of an afternoon tea, and these pack an extra hit of flavour to impress your family or guests.

MAKES 16 MINI SCONES

250g (9oz) self-raising flour, plus extra for dusting

1 tsp baking powder

25g (1oz) caster sugar

40g (1½oz) Stork® block

2 tbsp freeze-dried raspberry pieces

Zest of ½ lemon and 1 tbsp lemon juice

1 egg

100–175ml (3½–6fl oz) milk

1. Preheat the oven to 220°C/425°F/Gas Mark 7. Set out a baking sheet.
2. Place the flour, baking powder and sugar in a bowl. Add the Stork® and rub in until the mixture resembles fine breadcrumbs.
3. Stir in the raspberry pieces, lemon zest and juice.
4. Beat the egg and milk together, reserve 1 tablespoon for the glaze, then gradually add the remainder to the flour mixture, beating until you have a soft dough.
5. Turn the dough onto a floured work surface and knead gently until just smooth. Do not overwork it.
6. Pat the dough into a circle about 2cm (¾ inch) thick. Using a 4cm (1½ inch) cutter, stamp out 16 circles, lightly kneading and reshaping the trimmings to get the right number.
7. Place the scones on the baking sheet and bake for 8 minutes, until risen and golden. Serve warm with cream and jam.

Spinach, Red Pepper and Cheese Scones

Cheese scones are always irresistible, but with the addition of peppers and spinach, they become almost a complete meal. Try them for lunch, just broken open and spread with a little Stork®.

MAKES 8

225g (8oz) self-raising flour, plus extra for dusting

½ tsp salt

Good pinch of mustard powder

50g (2oz) Stork® block

50g (2oz) baby spinach leaves, very finely chopped

50g (2oz) Cheddar cheese, grated

1 roasted and peeled red pepper, finely chopped

150ml (5fl oz) milk

1. Preheat the oven to 220°C/425°F/Gas Mark 7. Set out a baking sheet.
2. Place the flour, salt and mustard in a bowl, then rub in the Stork® until the mixture resembles breadcrumbs. Add the spinach, cheese and red pepper and mix well. Pour in the milk and mix with a knife until a soft dough forms.
3. Turn the dough onto a lightly floured work surface, knead gently and shape into a circle about 3cm (1¼ inches) thick. Place on the baking sheet and score into 8 triangles.
4. Bake for 15–20 minutes, until golden brown and the scone ring sounds hollow when tapped on the bottom. Serve warm or cold.

Stork®'s recipe booklets were simple, eye-catching and fail-safe – a winning formula for successful baking, like these tempting scones.

STORK®
At the Heart of Home Baking™
All in one cookery

Blue Cheese and Sage Scones

The flavour combination in these scones makes them perfect for a stylish and tasty lunch, or the base of a smart canapé, topped with extra cheese and some red onion chutney perhaps.

MAKES 8

250g (9oz) self-raising flour, plus extra for dusting

1 tsp bicarbonate of soda

½ tsp salt

50g (2oz) Stork® block

120g (4½oz) blue cheese (Stilton or Roquefort), crumbled

6 sage leaves, very finely chopped

175ml (6fl oz) buttermilk

1. Preheat the oven to 220°C/425°F/Gas Mark 7. Set out a baking sheet.
2. Place the flour, bicarbonate of soda and salt in a bowl. Add the Stork® and rub in until the mixture resembles breadcrumbs.
3. Stir in the cheese and sage, then add the buttermilk and mix with a knife until a soft dough forms.
4. Turn the dough onto a floured work surface and knead lightly until smooth.
5. Roll out the dough to a thickness of 3cm (1¼ inches), then use a 10cm (4 inch) round cutter to stamp out 8 circles. Place them on the baking sheet and dust with flour.
6. Bake for 15–20 minutes, until golden brown and the scones sound hollow when tapped on the bottom. Serve warm or cold.

This 1954 advertisement emphasised the delicious taste of Stork®, a world away from the utilitarian wartime product.

Fresh, creamy goodness in every taste...
Naturally—it's Stork!

Classic Muffins

In just three simple steps from mixing bowl to oven you can have magical muffins on the table. This recipe is also highly adaptable, and you can add your own flavour combinations.

MAKES 12

350g (12oz) self-raising flour, sifted

1 tsp baking powder

75g (3oz) light soft brown sugar

75g (3oz) Stork® spread, melted

2 eggs, beaten

300ml (10fl oz) milk

1. Preheat the oven to 200°C/400°F/Gas Mark 6. Line a 12-hole muffin tray with paper cases.
2. Place all the ingredients in a large bowl and beat well.
3. Spoon the mixture into the paper cases and bake for 20–25 minutes.
4. Allow the muffins to sit in the tray for 3–4 minutes before transferring them to a wire rack to cool. Serve warm.

VARIATIONS

The following may be added to the basic batter at step 2, and the toppings added just before baking.

Berry muffins: 225g (8oz) blueberries or mixed wild berries.

Chocolate and hazelnut muffins: 75g (3oz) chocolate chips, 50g (2oz) chopped hazelnuts. Topping: About 2 tablespoons light brown sugar mixed with 1 teaspoon ground cinnamon.

Courgette and bacon muffins: Omit the sugar from the basic muffin mixture and add 1 small grated courgette, 6 cooked and chopped bacon rashers, salt, pepper and 1 tablespoon chopped chives. Topping: 50g (2oz) grated Cheddar cheese.

Blue Monster Muffins

Get the kids into the kitchen and make a batch of these fun monster muffins. They'll love helping out, and can be encouraged to use their imagination to create other fun faces too.

MAKES 12

100g (4oz) Stork® spread

100g (4oz) sugar

2 eggs

150g (5oz) flour

1 tsp baking powder

Pinch of salt

50ml (2fl oz) milk

75g (3oz) chocolate chips

120g (4½oz) Mini Chocolate Chip Cookies

FOR THE DECORATION

75g (3oz) desiccated coconut (ideally, extra coarse)

Blue food colouring

100g (4oz) marzipan

100g (4oz) icing sugar

1–2 tsp water

1. Preheat the oven to 200°C/400°F/Gas Mark 6. Line a 12-hole muffin tray with paper cases.
2. Cream the Stork® and sugar in a bowl until smooth, then beat in the eggs one at a time.
3. Combine the flour, baking powder and salt in a separate bowl and briefly whisk together.
4. Alternately beat the milk and flour into the egg mixture a bit at a time.
5. Set aside 24 chocolate chips, then mix the remainder into the batter.
6. Set aside 6 mini cookies, coarsely chop or crumble the rest and mix them into the batter.
7. Spoon the batter into the prepared tray and bake for 20–25 minutes, until a cocktail stick inserted in the middle of the muffins comes out clean. Allow to cool.
8. Meanwhile, place the coconut in a bowl, add 1–2 drops of blue food colouring and mash with a fork.
9. Break the marzipan into 24 equal pieces and roll them into 'eyeballs'. Push a chocolate chip into each eyeball to form the pupil.
10. Put the icing sugar into a bowl, add 1–2 drops of blue food colouring and the water (a bit at a time) and mix to form a paste.
11. Spread this icing over the muffins, then sprinkle with the coloured coconut. Stick the marzipan eyes to the muffins using a little icing. Set aside to dry.
12. For the mouth, make a shallow cut straight across each muffin about 1cm (½ inch) in from the curved front edge. Slice into this horizontally and lift out the wedge. Carefully cut the reserved cookies in half and stick one half, with the curved edge to the front, into each Blue Monster's mouth.

Gluten-free Blueberry and Lemon Buns

What could be simpler than these moist, fruit-packed buns? They're so tasty that no one will believe they are gluten-free. To ring the changes, add raspberries or dried fruit instead of blueberries.

Gf

MAKES 12

150g (5oz) gluten-free self-raising flour

2 tsp gluten-free baking powder

75g (3oz) caster sugar

120ml (4fl oz) milk

1 large egg

100g (4oz) Stork® spread

Grated zest of ½ lemon

150g (5oz) blueberries

1. Preheat the oven to 200°C/400°F/Gas Mark 6. Line a 12-hole bun tray with paper cases.
2. Place all the ingredients, apart from the blueberries, in a bowl and beat for 1–2 minutes, until just smooth.
3. Stir in the blueberries, then divide the mixture equally between the paper cases.
4. Bake for 18–20 minutes, or until the buns are risen and golden brown.
5. Leave to cool in the tray for 10 minutes before transferring to a wire rack to cool.

Gluten-free White Bread

This simple recipe makes the best-ever gluten-free bread. It will keep well in the bread bin for a day or two, and also toasts well.

Gf

MAKES A 450G (1LB) LOAF

350g (12oz) gluten-free flour
4 tbsp Stork® spread
1½ tsp easy-blend yeast
1 tsp caster sugar
1 tsp salt
1 tsp xanthan gum
250ml (8fl oz) milk
1 large egg
1 tsp vinegar
Vegetable oil, for greasing

1. Line a 450g (1lb) loaf tin with non-stick baking paper
2. Place the flour, Stork®, yeast, sugar, salt and xanthan gum in a large bowl and rub together until the mixture resembles breadcrumbs.
3. In a separate bowl, mix the milk, egg and vinegar together with a fork, then stir into the flour to give a soft dropping consistency.
4. Spoon the mixture into the prepared tin and level the surface. Cover loosely with oiled clingfilm and leave to rise in a warm place for about 45–60 minutes, or until it has risen to just above the top of the tin.
5. Preheat the oven to 200°C/400°F/Gas Mark 6, then bake the loaf for 30–40 minutes, or until golden brown and it sounds hollow when tapped on the base. Transfer to a wire rack to cool completely.

Vegan Wheaten Bread

Made without eggs or dairy products, this is a quick and easy loaf to make every day. It's dense and moist, similar to soda bread, and great sliced and served with Stork®.

MAKES A 900G (2LB) LOAF

50g (2oz) Stork® block, plus extra for brushing

250g (9oz) wholemeal flour

250g (9oz) plain flour

100g (4oz) rolled oats, plus extra for sprinkling

1½ tsp bicarbonate of soda

1 tsp salt

300ml (10fl oz) oat or soya yoghurt

1 tbsp maple syrup

250–300 ml (8–10fl oz) oat or soya milk

1. Preheat the oven to 230°C/450°F/Gas Mark 8. Brush a 900g (2lb) loaf tin with melted Stork® and line the bottom and sides with non-stick baking paper.
2. Place the flours, oats, bicarbonate of soda and salt in a bowl. Add the Stork® and rub in until the mixture resembles breadcrumbs.
3. Combine the yoghurt and maple syrup in a separate bowl, then stir into the flour with 250ml (8fl oz) of the milk, adding a little extra if needed to make a soft dough.
4. Pour the mixture into the prepared tin, smooth the surface and sprinkle with a few extra oats.
5. Bake the loaf for 10 minutes, then lower the temperature to 200°C/400°F/Gas Mark 6 and bake for a further 25–30 minutes, until golden and firm to the touch, and the base sounds hollow when tapped.

Notes: This bread keeps for 3–4 days in a plastic bag.

VARIATION

For an even more delicious loaf, add a few chopped walnuts, sesame seeds or sunflower seeds to the basic dough.

Vegan Pecan Muffins

These are perfect for breakfast, for a packed lunch, or just with a cup of coffee. Use whatever plant milk you like, but a nut milk will certainly complement the other flavours.

MAKES 10

100g (4oz) plain flour
120g (4½oz) wholemeal flour
½ tsp ground cinnamon
½ tsp ground mixed spice
50g (2oz) Stork® block
2 tsp baking powder
1 tsp bicarbonate of soda
150g (5oz) caster sugar
100ml (3½fl oz) soya yoghurt
1 tbsp maple syrup
150ml (5fl oz) soya, oat or nut milk
50g (2oz) chopped pecans
12 whole shelled pecans

1. Preheat the oven to 200°C/400°F/Gas Mark 6. Line a muffin tray with 10 paper cases.
2. Place the flours and spices in a large bowl. Add the Stork® and rub in until the mixture resembles breadcrumbs. Stir in the baking powder, bicarbonate of soda and sugar.
3. Combine the yoghurt, maple syrup and milk in a separate bowl, then stir into the flour bowl along with the chopped pecans to give a soft dropping consistency.
4. Divide the mixture equally between the paper cases and top each with a whole pecan. Bake for 18–20 minutes, until the centre is just firm to the touch. Transfer to a wire rack to cool.

Vegan Banana Bread with Sticky Toffee Sauce

This scrumptious banana bread is both vegan and gluten-free, but so good that everyone will want to eat it.

SERVES 12

75g (3oz) Stork® block, plus extra for brushing

3 bananas (2 mashed and 1 cut in half lengthways)

100ml (3½fl oz) unsweetened soya milk

1 tbsp lemon juice

225g (8oz) gluten-free self-raising flour

½ tsp gluten-free baking powder

½ tsp ground cinnamon

250g (9oz) light muscovado sugar

2 tbsp maple syrup

1 tsp vanilla extract

FOR THE TOFFEE SAUCE

50g (2oz) dark muscovado sugar

3 tbsp maple syrup

1 tbsp water

1. Preheat the oven to 180°C/350°F/Gas Mark 4. Brush a 900g (2lb) loaf tin with melted Stork®, and line the bottom with non-stick baking paper.
2. Lay the halved banana, cut side down, in the bottom of the tin.
3. Place the soya milk and lemon juice in a large bowl and leave for 2 minutes.
4. Sift the flour, baking powder and cinnamon over the milk, then add the sugar, Stork®, maple syrup, vanilla and mashed bananas. Mix together with an electric whisk until evenly blended.
5. Pour the batter into the prepared tin and bake for 1–1¼ hours, or until a skewer inserted into the middle comes out clean.
6. Leave to cool in the tin for 5 minutes, then turn onto a wire rack to cool.
7. To make the toffee sauce, gently heat the sugar, maple syrup and water together in a pan. Drizzle over the cake while it's still warm.

Muffins have long been a popular teatime treat, and this advertisement from the 1970s aimed to encourage children to make their own – with a bit of help from Mum, of course.

ALL IN ONE COOKERY

Ingredients: 85g(3oz)*Stork. 350g(12oz)self raising flour, sieved. 1 teaspoon baking powder. 85g(3oz) caster sugar. 100g(3oz) chocolate chips. 2 eggs, medium. 300ml (½pint) milk. Rind of one orange. How: Mix everything in bowl. Fill papercases with mixture and put in muffin tins. Sprinkle more choc chips on top. Allow Mum to bake in pre-heated oven. (200°c, 400°f, Gas mark 6) for 20–25 minutes. Have picture taken with muffins before eating them all. (Give one to Mum for helping).

The Stork Cookery Service

2 Large Cakes

Victoria Sandwich Cake

Long known as the nation's favourite cake, the Victoria sponge in this recipe first featured in All about Sandwich Cakes, Sponges and Swiss Rolls, *a leaflet produced by the Stork® Cookery Service in 1952. It's the perfect treat for afternoon tea.*

SERVES 6–8

100g (4oz) Stork® spread, plus extra for brushing

100g (4oz) caster sugar

2 eggs

100g (4oz) self-raising flour, sifted

FOR FILLING AND DUSTING

Raspberry jam

Icing sugar

1. Preheat the oven to 180°C/350°F/Gas Mark 4. Brush a deep 18cm (7 inch) sponge tin with melted Stork®, then line the bottom with a circle of non-stick baking paper.
2. Cream the Stork® and sugar together in a bowl until very light and fluffy.
3. Beat in the eggs one at a time, adding a little of the sifted flour with the second.
4. Fold in the remaining flour, then tip the mixture into the prepared tin and smooth the top with a knife. Bake for 25–30 minutes, until the surface is golden and springy.
5. Turn the sponge out of the tin and cool on a wire rack.
6. When completely cold, cut the sponge in half horizontally. Spread the bottom half with raspberry jam and place the remaining half sponge on top.
7. Dust the surface of the cake with icing sugar. If you want make this look a little more special, place a paper doily on top and sift the icing sugar over that. Lift off carefully to leave a pretty pattern.

VARIATIONS

See Appendix, page 217.

Irish Coffee Cake

This is a seriously good, grown-up coffee cake. Doused with a whiskey syrup, it's also good enough to serve as a dessert.

Serves 8

100g (4oz) Stork® spread, plus extra for brushing

100g (4oz) superfine sponge flour

125g (4½oz) caster sugar

2 eggs, beaten

2 tsp instant coffee dissolved in 2 tbsp hot water, then cooled

150ml (5fl oz) double cream

1 tbsp Irish whiskey

Coffee/liqueur chocolates, to serve

For the whiskey syrup

150ml (5fl oz) water

1 tbsp instant coffee

50g (2oz) caster sugar

2 tbsp Irish whiskey

1. Preheat the oven to 180°C/350°F/Gas Mark 4. Brush a 23cm (9 inch) ring tin with melted Stork®.
2. Place the Stork®, flour, sugar, eggs and coffee in a bowl and beat thoroughly for 1–2 minutes, until smooth and light.
3. Pour the mixture into the prepared tin and bake for 35–40 minutes, until risen and springy to the touch. Turn the cake out of the tin and cool on a wire rack.
4. To make the syrup, place the water, coffee and sugar in a small pan and heat gently until the sugar has dissolved. Bring to the boil, simmer for 5 minutes, then remove from the heat and stir in the 2 tablespoons of whiskey.
5. Place the cake back in the tin and prick all over with a skewer. Spoon the syrup over the cake and leave to soak in for about 30 minutes.
6. Transfer the cake to a serving plate. Whip the cream with the remaining whiskey until it just holds its shape, then spread all over the cake. Fill the centre of the ring with the chocolates.

Chocolate Swirl Cake

Taken from Teatime with Stork, *produced by the Stork® Cookery Service in the 1950s, this lovely cake is made with lots of melted chocolate added to the batter to make it moist and rich. It's ideal for a birthday celebration, or just enjoy it with a cup of tea.*

SERVES 8

175g (6oz) Stork® spread, plus extra for brushing

225g (8oz) plain flour

1½ tsp baking powder

Pinch of salt

2 rounded tbsp cocoa powder

4 tbsp boiling water

175g (6oz) dark chocolate (60% cocoa solids)

175g (6oz) caster sugar

4 tbsp golden syrup

3 eggs

1 tbsp milk

Walnut halves and quarters, to decorate

FOR THE CHOCOLATE RUM ICING

100g (4oz) dark or milk chocolate

450g (1lb) icing sugar

175g (6oz) Stork® spread

4 tbsp rum or 4 tbsp milk and ½ tsp rum extract

1. Preheat the oven to 150°C/300°F/Gas Mark 2. Line the bottom and sides of an 18cm (7 inch) cake tin with a double thickness of non-stick baking paper and brush with melted Stork®.
2. Sift the flour, baking powder and salt together into a bowl.
3. Combine the cocoa and water in a cup, blend smoothly, then cool.
4. Break up the chocolate and place in a heatproof bowl set over a pan of simmering water. Allow to melt, then cool a little.
5. Cream the Stork®, sugar and syrup together until light and fluffy, then beat in the cocoa paste and melted chocolate.
6. Beat the eggs in one at a time, adding a little sifted flour with each of the last two. Fold in the remaining flour and the milk.
7. Pour the mixture into the prepared tin and bake for 1¾–2½ hours, until a skewer inserted in the centre comes out clean. Turn the cake out of the tin and cool on a wire rack.
8. To make the icing, break up the chocolate and melt as in step 4. Set aside to cool a little.
9. Sift the icing sugar into a bowl. Place half in a separate bowl, add the Stork® and beat until light and fluffy. Add the remaining icing sugar and the rum, then beat again until light and fluffy. Set aside about 1 rounded tablespoon for decoration, then beat the melted chocolate into the remaining icing.
10. When the cake is cold, cut in half horizontally, fill with half the icing and sandwich together. Spread the remaining icing over the top, swirling a pattern with the tip of a knife. Arrange a ring of quartered walnuts in the centre of the cake. Add dots of the reserved icing around the edge and press a walnut half on each one.

Battenberg Cake

Anyone who enjoys marzipan will love this cake. It's fun to make and impressive to serve for afternoon tea.

SERVES 8

100g (4oz) Stork® spread, plus extra for brushing

100g (4oz) caster sugar

2 eggs

100g (4oz) self-raising flour, sifted

Red food colouring

3 tbsp apricot jam plus 2 tbsp water, boiled together and sieved

Icing sugar, for dusting

450g (1lb) ready-made almond paste

FOR THE DECORATION

Glacé cherries

Angelica leaves

1. Preheat the oven to 180°C/350°F/Gas Mark 4. Brush a 28 x 18cm (11 x 7 inch) Swiss roll tin with melted Stork®, and line the bottom and sides with non-stick baking paper. Make a partition of well-greased cardboard down the centre.

2. Cream the Stork® and sugar together in a bowl until light and fluffy. Beat in the eggs one at a time, adding a little of the sifted flour with the second egg. Fold in the remaining flour.

3. Transfer half the mixture to a separate bowl and add a dot of red food colouring, dropping it from a skewer or cocktail stick. Mix well, adding more colouring a dot at a time until you have your preferred shade of pink.

4. Place the two cake mixtures in the prepared tin on either side of the partition. Smooth evenly. Bake for 25–35 minutes, until a skewer inserted in the centre comes out clean. Turn the cake onto a wire rack, peel off the paper and leave to cool.

5. When the cake is cold, trim the edges, then cut lengthways into four strips (two pink and two white). Put a pink and a white strip side by side, spread the inside edges with some of the hot jam and press together to join. Repeat this with the other two strips. Brush the surface of one joined cake with the sieved jam and sit the other joined cake on top, making sure that the pink and white colours alternate.

6. Lightly dust a work surface with icing sugar, then roll out the almond paste to form a rectangle large enough to wrap around the cake. Brush lightly with sieved jam. Place the cake on top and wrap the paste around it. Trim the ends with a sharp knife so that the squared ends of the cake are exposed.

7. Flute the top long edges by pinching the paste at intervals between finger and thumb. Decorate with glacé cherries and angelica leaves.

By the time this advertisement was produced around 1960, successful baking was synonymous with Stork®.

Light and Easy Baking

Swiss Roll

Don't be afraid of making a Swiss roll; our step-by-step instructions – from All about Sandwich Cakes, Sponges and Swiss Rolls, *produced by the Stork® Cookery Service in 1952 – show you just how quick and easy it is, and the result is really impressive.*

SERVES 6

50g (2oz) Stork® spread, plus extra for brushing

100g (4oz) caster sugar, plus extra for sprinkling and dusting

2 eggs

100g (4oz) self-raising flour

2 tbsp jam

1. Preheat the oven to 200°C/400°F/Gas Mark 6. Brush a 28 x 18cm (11 x 7 inch) Swiss roll tin with melted Stork®, and line the bottom and sides with non-stick baking paper.
2. **All-in-one method**: Place all the ingredients in a bowl and beat until smooth.
   Creaming method: Cream the Stork® and sugar until light and fluffy. Beat in the eggs one at a time, adding a little of the sifted flour with the second. Fold in the remaining flour.
3. Spread the batter evenly in the prepared tin and bake for 10–12 minutes, until springy to the touch.
4. Meanwhile, cut a sheet of non-stick baking paper 2.5cm (1 inch) larger all round than the Swiss roll tin and dust with caster sugar.
5. When the Swiss roll is ready, turn it onto the sugared paper and carefully peel off the lining paper (see opposite).
6. Neaten the cake by cutting a 5mm (¼ inch) strip off all the edges.
7. Warm the jam, then quickly spread it over the cake, leaving a clear 5mm (¼ inch) border around the edge.
8. With the short edge nearest to you, fold over about 1cm (½ inch) of it and hold it in place with one hand.
9. Using your free hand, lift the paper and use it to help you continue rolling the cake away from you until it is completely rolled up. Hold in position for a few moments, still covered with the paper, then place on a wire rack to cool.
10. When cold, remove the paper and sprinkle the Swiss roll with caster sugar.

Note: If you want to store the cake for future use, roll it up and open-freeze it on a plate, then wrap in clingfilm and foil and return it to the freezer. Unwrap before defrosting.

VARIATION

Cream-filled Swiss roll: Roll up the cake in the same way as above, but omit any filling at all. When it is cold and set, unroll it very carefully to avoid cracking, and spread it with whipped cream. Roll up again without using the sugared paper. The cake must be absolutely cold when you do this, or the cream will melt.

Lemon and Elderflower Drizzle Cake

This is such a lovely cake to serve to friends and family in the spring or summer. For a final flourish, why not top with edible fresh flowers, such as roses, pansies or honeysuckle?

SERVES 12

350g (12oz) Stork® spread, plus extra for brushing
350g (12oz) self-raising flour
1 tsp baking powder
350g (12oz) caster sugar
6 eggs
2 tbsp elderflower cordial
Finely grated zest of 2 lemons
Edible flowers, to decorate (optional)

FOR THE SYRUP

Juice of 1 lemon, strained
1 tbsp elderflower cordial
50g (2oz) caster sugar

FOR THE FILLING

100g (4oz) icing sugar
40g (1½oz) Stork® spread
1–2 tsp elderflower cordial
3–4 tbsp lemon curd

FOR THE GLACÉ ICING

50g (2oz) icing sugar
Lemon juice

1. Preheat the oven to 180°C/350°F/Gas Mark 4. Brush two 20cm (8 inch) cake tins with melted Stork® and line the bottom with non-stick baking paper.

2. Sift the flour and baking powder into a large bowl, add the remaining cake ingredients and beat until smooth.

3. Spoon the batter into the prepared tins and bake for 30–40 minutes, or until a skewer inserted in the centre comes out clean. Turn the cakes out of the tins and cool on a wire rack.

4. To make the syrup, put the lemon juice, cordial and sugar in a saucepan and heat gently until the sugar has dissolved.

5. Whilst the cakes are still warm, peel off the paper and turn them the right way up. Make a few deep holes in them with a skewer and drizzle the syrup over so that it soaks in.

6. To make the filling, place the icing sugar, Stork® and cordial in a bowl and mix well until smooth.

7. Slice the cakes in half horizontally. Spread the base half with one-third of the elderflower icing and one-third of the lemon curd. Top with the second layer of cake and repeat the layers of filling. Repeat with the third layer, finishing with the final layer of cake.

8. To make the glacé icing, mix the sugar with a little lemon juice and drizzle it over the top of the cake. Decorate with edible flowers, if liked.

Carrot Cake

Moist and rich, but not too sweet, carrot cake is everyone's favourite, and it's so simple and quick to make. Store it in the fridge and it will keep well for 3–4 days.

SERVES 16–20

225g (8oz) Stork® spread, plus extra for brushing

100g (4oz) plain flour

2 tsp ground cinnamon

1 tsp bicarbonate of soda

350g (12oz) caster sugar

4 eggs

175g (6oz) self-raising wholemeal flour

3 large carrots, peeled and grated

FOR THE TOPPING

200g (7oz) full-fat soft cream cheese

4 tbsp icing sugar

Juice and grated zest of ½ lemon

1. Preheat the oven to 180°C/350°F/Gas Mark 4. Brush a 23cm (9 inch) square cake tin with melted Stork®, and line the bottom with non-stick baking paper.
2. Sift the plain flour, cinnamon and bicarbonate into a large bowl. Add the remaining cake ingredients and beat thoroughly for 2–3 minutes.
3. Spoon the mixture into the prepared tin and bake for 60–80 minutes, until a skewer inserted in the centre comes out clean. Turn onto a wire rack and leave to cool before peeling off the paper.
4. To make the topping, beat the cream cheese in a bowl until smooth, then beat in the icing sugar, lemon juice and zest. Spread over the cold cake and cut into 16–20 squares.

It was in 1952 that Stork® published this booklet explaining everything the home baker needed to know about producing light and airy sponge cakes.

All about–
SANDWICH CAKES
SPONGES
& SWISS ROLLS
All about–
SANDWICH CAKES
SPONGES
SANDWICH CAKES
SPONGES
SWISS ROLLS

Orange Cake

The zest of a couple of oranges really boosts the flavour of the basic cake mixture given here, and by adding the juice to the buttercream, you have a particularly flavoursome teatime treat.

SERVES 8

100g (4oz) Stork® spread, plus extra for brushing

100g (4oz) caster sugar

Finely grated zest of 2 oranges

2 eggs

100g (4oz) self-raising flour, sifted

FOR THE FROSTING

Juice of 2 oranges

50g (2oz) Stork® spread

450g (1lb) icing sugar, sifted

FOR THE DECORATION

2 packets coloured wafer biscuits (optional)

Halved walnuts

Glacé cherries

1. Preheat the oven to 180°C/350°F/Gas Mark 4. Brush a 20cm (8 inch) sponge tin with melted Stork® and line the bottom with non-stick baking paper.
2. Cream the Stork® and sugar until light and fluffy, then beat in the orange zest.
3. Beat in the eggs one at a time, adding a little sifted flour with the second. Fold in the remaining flour.
4. Pour the batter into the prepared tin, smooth evenly and bake for 25–35 minutes, until a skewer inserted in the centre comes out clean. Turn onto a wire rack, peel off the paper and leave to cool.
5. To make the frosting, stir the orange juice and Stork® in a pan over a low heat until the Stork® has melted. Add half the icing sugar, stir over a low heat until dissolved, then bring to the boil and boil fairly fast for 5 minutes from the time the first bubbles appear around the sides. Remove, stir in remaining icing sugar and pour into a bowl. Beat until thick. Leave overnight or for several hours, until thick and firm. Beat again before using, adding 1–2 teaspoons hot water if too thick to spread.
6. When the cake is cold, cut in half horizontally and spread with half the frosting, using a palette knife dipped in hot water. Sandwich the two halves together, then cover the top and sides with the remaining frosting.
7. If you want to decorate the sides, cut the wafers into equal lengths the depth of the cake and stick them to the icing while it is still wet. Decorate the top with the walnuts and cherries.

Coffee Walnut Cake

Everyone loves a classic coffee and walnut cake, especially this one, which the Stork® Cookery Service first produced in the 1940s, so why not rustle one up for your nearest and dearest?

SERVES 8

175g (6oz) Stork® spread, plus extra for brushing

225g (8oz) plain flour

1½ tsp baking powder

175g (6oz) caster sugar

3 eggs

2 tbsp milk

75g (3oz) walnuts, chopped, plus extra halves to decorate

FOR THE COFFEE GLACÉ ICING

350g (12oz) icing sugar

1 tbsp instant coffee dissolved in 1 tbsp hot water

1½ tbsp warm water

1. Preheat the oven to 160°C/325°F/Gas Mark 3. Brush a deep 18cm (7 inch) round cake tin with melted Stork® and line with non-stick baking paper.
2. Sift the flour and baking powder together into a bowl.
3. In a separate bowl, cream the Stork® and sugar together until light and fluffy. Beat in the eggs one at a time, adding a little of the sifted flour with every egg after the first. Fold in the remaining flour.
4. Fold in the milk and chopped walnuts.
5. Place the mixture in the prepared tin and bake for 1½–2 hours. Rest in the tin for 2–3 minutes, then turn onto a wire rack and leave to cool.
6. To make the icing, sift the icing sugar into a bowl, then stir in the coffee. Stand the bowl in a saucepan and pour enough hot water around it to come halfway up the sides. Beat for 1–2 minutes over a low heat, but do not allow the icing to become more than lukewarm. It is the correct consistency when it coats the back of a spoon.
7. To decorate the cake, pour the icing over it and quickly spread it over the top and sides with a knife. Decorate with the walnut halves.

VARIATION

Chocolate marbled cake: Omit the chopped walnuts. Place half the mixture in separate bowl and gently fold in 1 rounded tablespoon sifted cocoa powder. Place the plain mixture and the chocolate mixture in layers in the prepared tin, then stir two or three times with a skewer to swirl them into each other. To decorate, omit the coffee from the icing and mix in 2½ tablespoons warm water. Swirl the icing over the cake and sprinkle the top with grated chocolate.

White Chocolate Cake with Strawberries

Topped with cream and fruit, this is the perfect cake to serve to friends on a lovely summer day.

SERVES 8

225g (8oz) Stork® spread, plus extra for brushing

225g (8oz) caster sugar

1 tsp vanilla extract

4 eggs

225g (8oz) self-raising flour, sifted, or plain flour plus 1 tsp baking powder, sifted

100g (4oz) white chocolate, finely grated

FOR THE FILLING

300ml (10fl oz) double cream

Few drops of vanilla extract

2 tbsp icing sugar

FOR THE DECORATION

500g (1lb 2oz) strawberries

20g (¾oz) blueberries

Few sprigs of mint

1. Preheat the oven to 180°C/350°F/Gas Mark 4. Brush two 20cm (8 inch) cake tins with melted Stork® and line the bottom with non-stick baking paper.
2. Cream the Stork® and caster sugar in a bowl until light and fluffy.
3. Beat in the vanilla, then the eggs one at a time.
4. Fold in the flour, then stir in the chocolate.
5. Divide the mixture between the prepared tins and bake for 25–30 minutes, until a skewer inserted in the centre comes out clean. Turn the cakes out of the tins and cool on a wire rack.
6. To prepare the filling, whip the cream until thick. Add the vanilla and icing sugar and mix thoroughly.
7. When the cakes are cold, peel off the paper. Spread one-third of the cream mixture over one cake and sit the other cake on top.
8. Carefully spread most of the remaining cream over the top, reserving some to pipe a decoration around the edge if you wish.
9. Arrange the strawberries and blueberries on top of the cake and decorate with the sprigs of mint.

Caraway and Lemon Loaf Cake

This is a wonderful old-time cake. The caraway seeds give a gentle, almost aniseed flavour that goes particularly well with the lemon zest and juice.

Serves 12

175g (6oz) Stork® spread
175g (6oz) caster sugar
175g (6oz) self-raising flour
3 large eggs
50g (2oz) ground almonds
Zest and juice 1 lemon
1 tbsp caraway seeds

1. Preheat the oven to 180°C/350°F/Gas Mark 4. Brush a 900g (2lb) loaf tin with melted Stork® and line with non-stick baking paper.
2. Place all the cake ingredients in a bowl and beat until smooth.
3. Tip the batter into the prepared tin and spread evenly. Bake for 1 hour, or until firm and golden, and a skewer inserted in the centre comes out clean.
4. Allow to cool in the tin for 10 minutes, then turn onto a wire rack to cool completely before slicing.

For generations, home cooks had been combining ingredients step by step, so Stork®'s all-in-one method for cakes, sauces, soups and suppers was an exciting development, as shown by this 1977 recipe booklet.

cooking
the
Stork
'all-in-one'
way

Cherry Cake

During the 1940s, when the Stork® Cookery Service first produced this recipe, comfort food was hard to come by, so this teatime treat was very popular. It remains a great favourite to this day, so keep this lovely bake in the cake tin, ready to serve whenever friends drop in.

SERVES 8

175g (6oz) Stork® spread, plus extra for brushing

225g (8oz) plain flour

1½ tsp baking powder

175g (6oz) caster sugar

3 eggs

1 tbsp milk

225g (8oz) glacé cherries, rinsed, dried and cut in half

1. Preheat the oven to 160°C/325°F/Gas Mark 3. Brush a deep 18cm (7 inch) round cake tin with melted Stork® and line with non-stick baking paper.
2. Sift the flour and baking powder together into a bowl.
3. Cream the Stork® and sugar together in a separate bowl until very light and fluffy. Beat in the eggs one at a time, adding a little of the sifted flour with every egg after the first. Fold in the remaining flour and the milk, half at a time. Finally, fold in the prepared cherries.
4. Place the mixture in the prepared tin and bake for 1½–1¾ hours. Leave in the tin for 2–3 minutes, then turn out, peel off the paper and cool on a wire rack.

VARIATIONS

Cherry coconut cake: Fold in 100g (4oz) desiccated coconut with the flour and milk.

Cherry almond cake: Fold in 50g (2oz) ground almonds with the flour and milk.

Produced in the 1960s, this booklet offered lots of ideas for feeding a family with quick and simple recipes, ranging from light breakfasts to speedy suppers.

CLOCK WISE
COOKING
with
STORK
FROM THE STORK COOKERY SERVICE

Rich Fruit Cake

Packed with fruit and nuts, this cake featured in Cakes for All Occasions*, first produced by the Stork® Cookery Service in 1949. It is perfect for celebrations, but there's no need to keep it just for special occasions; it's lovely to slice and serve whenever you fancy.*

SERVES 16

275g (10oz) Stork® spread, plus extra for brushing

350g (12oz) plain flour, plus extra if needed

Pinch of salt

1 rounded tsp ground mixed spice

275g (10oz) caster sugar or 275g (10oz) golden syrup

6 eggs

1 tsp each vanilla and almond extract

350g (12oz) sultanas

225g (8oz) currants

175g (6oz) raisins or dates

175g (6oz) chopped glacé cherries

100g (4oz) chopped mixed peel

100g (4oz) chopped blanched almonds

½ tsp bicarbonate of soda dissolved in 1 tsp milk

1. Preheat the oven to 150°C/300°F/Gas Mark 2. Brush a deep 23cm (9 inch) cake tin with melted Stork®, then line it with a double thickness of non-stick baking paper, standing it 2.5cm (1 inch) higher than the tin.
2. Sift the flour, salt and spice into a bowl.
3. Cream the Stork® and sugar in a separate bowl, then gradually beat in the eggs, vanilla and almond extracts, adding a little extra flour if the mixture begins to curdle.
4. Fold small amounts of the flour, fruit, peel and nuts alternately into the creamed mixture until they have all been added. Finally, fold in the bicarbonate and milk mixture.
5. Pour the batter into the prepared tin and bake for 4½ hours, until a skewer inserted in the centre comes out clean.
6. Allow to cool in the tin for 5 minutes, then turn out carefully, peel off the paper and finish cooling on a wire rack.
7. Ice and decorate as you wish.

While rationing of dried fruit ended in 1950, it was another three years before sugar became freely available. Stork celebrated by producing this leaflet, giving pride of place to its popular rich fruit cake.

ALL ABOUT
FRUIT
CAKES

Gluten-free Orange Polenta Cake

Ground almonds and polenta serve as a substitute for flour in this wonderfully moist cake that's drenched in an orange syrup.

Gf

SERVES 12

175g (6oz) Stork® spread, plus extra for brushing

200g (7oz) caster sugar

3 eggs, beaten

175g (6oz) ground almonds

100g (4oz) polenta

2 tsp gluten-free baking powder

Zest and juice of 2 oranges (5–6 tbsp juice)

Fresh fruit (orange slices, raspberries, blueberries, etc.), to decorate

FOR THE SYRUP

100g (4oz) caster sugar

100ml (3½fl oz) orange juice

1. Preheat the oven to 180°C/350°F/Gas Mark 4. Brush an 18cm (7 inch) round sponge tin with melted Stork® and line the bottom with non-stick baking paper.
2. Beat the Stork® and sugar together in a bowl until light and creamy, then beat in the eggs, ground almonds, polenta and baking powder. Stir in the orange zest and juice.
3. Pour the mixture into the prepared tin and bake for 25–30 minutes, or until just firm in the centre.
4. Meanwhile, make the syrup. Place the sugar and orange juice in a pan, stir and bring to the boil, then simmer for 3–4 minutes, until slightly syrupy.
5. Remove the cooked cake from the oven and, while it is still in the tin, pour over half the syrup. Set aside to cool.
6. Transfer the cake to a plate, decorate with fresh fruit and offer the remaining syrup in a jug for people to help themselves.

Vegan Lemon and Almond Cake

Everyone will be amazed that this is vegan. It contains no eggs or dairy, but is packed with flavour and wonderfully moist.

SERVES 12

300ml (10fl oz) almond milk
2 tbsp white wine vinegar
175g (6oz) Stork® block
200g (7oz) caster sugar
Zest of 1 lemon
300g (11oz) ground almonds
200g (7oz) self-raising flour
2 tsp baking powder
1 tbsp toasted flaked almonds, to decorate

FOR THE DRIZZLE

Juice of 1 lemon
2 tbsp caster sugar

FOR THE ICING

120g (4½oz) fondant icing sugar
Few drops of almond extract

1. Preheat the oven to 180°C/350°F/Gas Mark 4. Line a 900g (2lb) loaf tin or a 20cm (8 inch) round cake tin with non-stick baking paper.
2. Put the almond milk and vinegar in a jug and leave to stand for 5–10 minutes, until curdled.
3. Beat the Stork®, sugar and lemon zest together in a bowl until light and fluffy. Gradually beat in half the curdled milk and half the ground almonds and flour. Add the baking powder and the remaining flour, ground almonds and lemon zest, and beat to combine. It will be quite a wet mixture.
4. Pour the batter into the prepared tin and bake for 1 hour, or until the top is golden and a skewer inserted in the centre comes out clean.
5. Meanwhile, make the drizzle by mixing the lemon juice and sugar together in a bowl.
6. Allow the cake to cool in the tin for 10 minutes, then prick the cake all over the surface with a cocktail stick and pour the drizzle over it. Set aside until completely cold, then turn out of the tin, peel off the paper and transfer to a plate.
7. To make the icing, combine the fondant icing sugar in a bowl with the almond extract and enough water to make a very thick but pourable mixture. Drizzle this over the top of the cake and sprinkle with the flaked almonds.

Gluten-free and Vegan Avocado, Chocolate and Lime Cake

Yes, this cake really is made with mashed avocado, and it's in the icing too. You can't actually taste it, but you'll be amazed by the moistness and richness that it imparts.

Gf V

SERVES 8

120g (4½oz) Stork® spread, plus extra for brushing

175g (6oz) ripe avocado flesh

Zest of 1 lime

300g (11oz) light muscovado sugar

350g (12oz) self-raising gluten-free flour

375ml (13fl oz) soya milk

50g (2oz) cocoa powder

FOR THE FROSTING

100g (4oz) ripe avocado flesh

120g (4½oz) Stork® spread

25g (1oz) cocoa powder

Juice of 1 lime

300g (11oz) icing sugar

FOR DECORATION

2 limes

1. Preheat the oven to 180°C/350°F/Gas Mark 4. Brush two 18cm (7 inch) round sponge tins with melted Stork® and line the bottom with non-stick baking paper.
2. Mash the avocado in a large bowl until really smooth, then add the remaining cake ingredients. Beat until smooth.
3. Divide the batter equally between the prepared tins and bake for 25–30 minutes, until risen and just firm to the touch. Leave to cool in the tins for 10 minutes, then turn onto a wire rack and leave to cool completely.
4. To make the frosting, mash the avocado until really smooth, then press through a sieve into a clean bowl. Add the remaining ingredients and beat until smooth.
5. Use half the frosting to sandwich the two cakes together, and spread the other half on top.
6. To decorate, slice one of the limes, then cut each slice in half and arrange on the surface of the cake. Zest the remaining lime and sprinkle over the frosting.

Vegan Chocolate Fudge Cake

This recipe proves that you can have your cake and eat it too. By using Stork® block, dairy-free chocolate and almond milk, this cake is absolutely vegan, and absolutely delicious.

SERVES 12

200g (7oz) Stork® block, plus extra for brushing

275g (10oz) dark dairy-free chocolate

150g (5oz) caster sugar

150g (5oz) light muscovado sugar

1 tsp vanilla extract

200g (7oz) plain flour

1 tsp baking powder

200g (7oz) ground almonds

225ml (7½fl oz) almond milk

FOR THE ICING

200g (7oz) dark dairy-free chocolate

200g (7oz) Stork® block

400g (14oz) icing sugar

TO DECORATE

300g raspberries

Icing sugar, for dusting

1. Preheat the oven to 180°C/350°F/Gas Mark 4. Brush three 18cm (7 inch) round sponge tins with melted Stork® and line the bottom with non-stick baking paper.
2. Break the chocolate into a pan, add the Stork® and melt together over a gentle heat until smooth and combined.
3. Pour the chocolate mixture into a bowl and stir in both sugars and the vanilla. Fold in the flour, baking powder and ground almonds, then gradually stir in the milk.
4. Divide the mixture between the prepared tins and bake for 35 minutes, until springy to the touch. Set aside to cool completely in the tins.
5. To make the icing, melt the chocolate in a bowl set over a pan of simmering water, then allow to cool for 10 minutes.
6. Beat the Stork® and icing sugar together in a bowl until pale and creamy, then beat in the melted chocolate.
7. Turn the cakes out of the tins and peel off the paper. Sandwich them together with the icing, and spread a layer of icing on top.
8. Decorate with the raspberries and dust with icing sugar.

3
Small Cakes and Traybakes

White Chocolate Blondies

The ultimate treat to serve with a cup of coffee, these blonde brownies are simplicity itself to make.

MAKES 16

165g (5½oz) Stork® spread

175g (6oz) plain flour

1 tsp baking powder

50g (2oz) ground almonds

225g (8oz) light muscovado sugar

2 large eggs, beaten

1 tsp vanilla extract

175g (6oz) white chocolate, chopped

1. Preheat the oven to 180°C/350°F/Gas Mark 4. Brush a 20cm (8 inch) square shallow cake tin with melted Stork® and line the bottom and sides with non-stick baking paper.

2. Place all the ingredients, except the chocolate, in a bowl and beat until just smooth. Stir in the chocolate, then spread the mixture into the tin.

3. Bake in the centre of the oven for 30–35 minutes, or until a skewer inserted in the centre comes out just a little sticky: the mixture is best slightly undercooked so that it has a hint of chewiness in the centre, but it can be baked for another 5 minutes if you prefer a firmer texture.

4. Leave to cool for 10 minutes before turning onto a wire rack. Cut into 16 squares when cool.

Raspberry Blondies

These white chocolate squares filled with raspberries are melt in the mouth – in fact, even good enough to serve with a little cream as a dessert.

MAKES 12

100g (4oz) Stork® block, plus extra for brushing

200g (7oz) white chocolate, chopped

2 eggs

100g (4oz) caster sugar

125g (4½oz) plain flour

100g (4oz) fresh raspberries

1. Preheat the oven to 190°C/375°F/Gas Mark 5. Brush an 18cm (7 inch) square cake tin with melted Stork®, and line the bottom with non-stick baking paper.
2. Melt the Stork® in a pan, add half the chocolate and stir until nice and smooth.
3. Whisk the eggs and sugar together in a large bowl until creamy and slightly thickened.
4. Sift the flour into the bowl and fold in gently along with the melted chocolate mixture. Add half the remaining chopped chocolate and half the raspberries.
5. Carefully pour the batter into the prepared tin. Sprinkle the remaining chopped chocolate and raspberries over the top.
6. Bake for 35–45 minutes, until beautifully golden. Leave to cool before cutting into 12 squares.

Chocolate Brownies

The secret to a good brownie is not to overbake it. Take these ones out of the oven when still slightly soft in the centre so they are just a little squishy to eat.

MAKES 12

50g (2oz) Stork® spread, plus extra for brushing

100g (4oz) dark chocolate (60% cocoa solids)

3 eggs

225g (8oz) caster sugar

1 tsp vanilla extract

40g (1½oz) plain flour

25g (1oz) cocoa powder

1 tsp baking powder

50g (2oz) set natural yoghurt

50g (2oz) walnuts or pecans, finely chopped

1. Preheat the oven to 180°C/350°F/Gas Mark 4. Brush a 23cm (9 inch) square cake tin with melted Stork®.
2. Break the chocolate into a heatproof bowl, add the Stork® and set over a pan of simmering water until melted.
3. Put the eggs, sugar and vanilla in a large bowl and whisk until creamy and slightly thickened.
4. Sift the dry ingredients together, then add to the eggs along with the chocolate mixture, yoghurt and nuts. Mix gently.
5. Pour the batter into the prepared tin and bake for 45–50 minutes. Leave to cool before cutting into 12 squares.

From scones and traybakes to rich fruit cakes, the recipes in this Stork® booklet could all be made by combining the ingredients in one go.

STORK
ALL IN ONE
Cookery
The Stork
Cookery Service

Mango and Lime Cupcakes

Lime juice, soft mango and creamy yoghurt help to make these cupcakes really moist and fruity, ideal for keeping in the cake tin as a treat for all the family to enjoy.

MAKES 12

Juice and finely grated zest of 1 lime

100g (4oz) ready-to-eat dried mango, finely chopped, plus a little extra, finely sliced, for decoration

100g (4oz) natural yoghurt

150g (5oz) caster sugar

100g (4oz) Stork® spread

2 eggs

150g (5oz) plain flour

1½ tsp baking powder

FOR THE ICING

1 lime

100g (4oz) fondant icing sugar

1. Preheat the oven to 180°C/350°F/Gas Mark 4. Line a 12-hole deep cupcake tin with paper cases.
2. Place the lime zest and juice in a bowl and add all the other cake ingredients. Beat for 1–2 minutes, until just smooth.
3. Spoon the mixture equally into the paper cases and bake for 20–25 minutes, or until just firm to the touch. Allow the cakes to cool for 10 minutes, then transfer to a wire rack to cool.
4. To make the icing, use a potato peeler to pare the zest of the lime, then slice into fine shreds. Squeeze the juice. Put the icing sugar in a bowl and mix in enough of the lime juice to make a thick pouring consistency.
5. Pour the icing over the cooled cakes, then decorate with the finely sliced lime zest and extra mango.

Note: These cupcakes will keep for 3–4 days in an airtight container.

As this 1960s illustration conveys, hearth and home have a timeless appeal, and the comforts of a cosy chair and a cake freshly baked with Stork® are irresistible.

ENJOY LIFE
WITH
STORK

Rich Small Cakes

This is such an adaptable recipe – it's based on the weight of eggs, so you can multiply the ingredients to make as many cakes as you want, and also add whatever flavourings you like.

MAKES 12

Stork® spread
2 eggs
Caster sugar
Self-raising flour

1. Preheat the oven to 190°C/375°F/Gas Mark 5. Brush a 12-hole bun tin with melted Stork®, or line it with paper cases.
2. Weigh a bowl and zero the figure. Crack the eggs into it and note the weight.
3. Zero the figure again, then measure out the same weight of Stork®, sugar and flour, zeroing the figure each time.
4. Beat the ingredients thoroughly, then spoon the mixture into the prepared tin and bake for 12–15 minutes. Transfer to a wire rack to cool.

Children's tea, afternoon tea or Sunday tea – all were catered for in the 1950s collection of recipes opposite, and there were also ideas for decorating the tea table.

VARIATIONS

Add the following to the basic batter, but add the decorations after baking.

Queen cakes: 25g (1oz) chopped candied lemon peel and 1 teaspoon vanilla extract.

Orange cakes: Juice and grated zest of 1 orange. Decorate with strips of orange zest.

Cherry cakes: 50g (2oz) chopped glacé cherries. Decorate each cake with half a cherry.

Lemon cakes: Juice and grated zest of 1 lemon. Decorate with candied lemon peel.

Madeleines: Bake in dariole moulds brushed with melted Stork®. Turn out, brush with warm apricot jam and roll in desiccated coconut. Stick a cherry on top of each one.

Spice cakes: Add ½ teaspoon ground mixed spice, and put half a blanched almond in each paper case before adding the batter. Serve upside down.

TeaTime
with Stork

Eccles Cakes

Flaky pastry packed with currants and spice is a wonderful combination, especially if eaten fresh on the day of baking. This recipe originally featured in Stork's Tour of Britain's Cooking, *produced by the Stork® Cookery Service in 1950. For a change, try eating these classic cakes with a chunk of Cheshire cheese.*

MAKES 16

1 quantity chilled Rough Puff Pastry (see page 142)
25g (1oz) Stork® spread
1 tbsp soft brown sugar
100g (4oz) currants
50g (2oz) mixed peel
½ tsp ground mixed spice
Flour, for dusting

FOR THE GLAZE

Milk
Caster sugar

1. While the pastry is chilling, make the filling. Melt the Stork® in a saucepan, then stir in the sugar, currants, peel and spice. Leave to cool.
2. Lightly flour a work surface and roll the pastry into a rectangle about 5mm (¼ inch) thick. Fold into thirds to make a small, thick block, turn 90 degrees and roll and fold again. Repeat this once more.
3. Preheat the oven to 220°C/425°F/Gas Mark 7. Set out a baking sheet.
4. Roll out the pastry to the thickness of a £1 coin. Using a well-floured 9cm (3½ inch) plain cutter, stamp out 16 circles.
5. Place 2 teaspoons of the filling in the centre of each circle. Dampen the edges with water, then gather together over the filling and press to seal.
6. Turn the cakes over so that the sealed side is underneath. Gently roll each one into a round flat shape about 1cm (½ inch) thick and place on the baking sheet. Chill for at least 15 minutes.
7. Make three slits across the top of each cake. Brush with milk and sprinkle thickly with caster sugar.
8. Bake for 20–25 minutes, until golden, then cool on a wire rack.

Note: Eccles cakes freeze well either before or after baking.

Flapjacks

Nothing could be simpler to make than flapjacks. They're packed with good things, taste great and the oats they contain are a source of slow-release energy, so they'll keep you going for longer. The perfect snack!

MAKES 12

100g (4oz) Stork® spread, plus extra for brushing

100g (4oz) golden syrup

50g (2oz) soft brown sugar

175g (6 oz) rolled oats

Chocolate, for decoration (optional)

1. Preheat the oven to 180°C/350°F/Gas Mark 4. Brush a shallow 18cm (7 inch) baking tin with melted Stork®.
2. Put the Stork®, syrup and sugar in a saucepan and melt over a gentle heat.
3. Add the rolled oats and mix thoroughly.
4. Spread the mixture into the prepared tin and bake for 25–30 minutes. Cut into 12 equal pieces and leave in the tin until cold.
5. If liked, melt some chocolate and drizzle it over the flapjacks, or dip the ends in it.

Ginger and Marmalade Traybake

Difficult, we know, but if you can resist tucking into this moist cake for a day or two, it will become stickier and taste even better.

MAKES 12–25 SQUARES

500g (1lb 2oz) plain flour

2 tbsp ground ginger

1 tbsp baking powder

1 tsp bicarbonate of soda

1 tsp salt

250g (9oz) dark muscovado sugar

175g (6oz) Stork® spread

175g (6oz) golden syrup

175g (6oz) orange marmalade, plus 3 tbsp extra for spreading

300ml (10fl oz) milk

1 egg

1. Preheat the oven to 150°C/300°F/Gas Mark 2. Line a 28 x 23cm (11 x 9 inch) baking tray with non-stick baking paper.
2. Sift the flour, ginger, baking powder, bicarbonate of soda and salt into a bowl.
3. Place the sugar, Stork®, syrup and marmalade in a pan and heat until the Stork® has just melted. Don't allow it to get too hot. Remove from the heat, stir in the milk, then beat in the egg. Pour this mixture into the dry ingredients and beat together.
4. Tip the batter immediately into the prepared tray and bake for 50–60 minutes, until firm to the touch. Allow to cool for 10 minutes, then turn onto a wire rack and allow to cool completely.
5. Turn the sponge right side up, spread the top with the extra marmalade and cut into 12–25 squares, depending on your preferred size.

Toffee Apple Ring

A cross between a hot cross bun and a strudel, this ring has a heavenly cinnamon and apple filling, and the melted toffee drizzle makes it completely irresistible.

MAKES 10 SLICES

225g (8oz) strong white flour, plus extra for dusting

½ tsp salt

25g (1oz) Stork® spread

1 x 7g sachet easy-blend yeast

1 tsp caster sugar

100ml (3½fl oz) warm milk

1 egg, beaten

FOR THE FILLING

15g (½oz) Stork® spread, melted

50g (2 oz) soft dark brown sugar

2 tsp ground cinnamon

1–2 apples, peeled, cored and finely diced

FOR THE TOPPING

100g (4oz) creamy toffees

2 tbsp milk

Flaked almonds

1. Line a baking sheet with non-stick baking paper.
2. Place the flour and salt in a bowl. Rub in the Stork® until the mixture resembles breadcrumbs, then stir in the yeast and sugar. Add the milk and egg and mix to a dough with a palette knife.
3. Turn onto a lightly floured work surface and knead for 10 minutes.
4. Roll the dough into a 23 x 30cm (9 x 12 inch) rectangle. Brush with the melted Stork®, then sprinkle with the sugar, cinnamon and apple. Roll up lightly from the long side and seal the ends together to form a ring.
5. Place on the prepared baking sheet and use a sharp knife to make 8 slashes in the top of the dough. Gently ease the slashes open, then cover the ring with clingfilm and leave to rise in a warm place for 30–45 minutes, until doubled in size.
6. Preheat the oven to 190°C/375°F/Gas Mark 5, then bake the ring for 30–35 minutes, until golden and risen.
7. To make the topping, gently melt the toffees and milk together in a saucepan. Allow to cool until thick, then spoon over the baked ring and sprinkle the almonds on top.

In the 1950s many people still recalled the shortages of the war years, so illustrations like this, which depicted sweet treats of many different types, were very appealing.

FROM THE STORK COOKERY SERVICE

Gluten-free Raspberry and Coconut Slice

A lovely shortbread base topped with jam and a coconut meringue makes this slice perfect for afternoon tea or adding to lunchboxes, and will keep well in a cake tin for up to a week.

Gf

MAKES 16 SQUARES

100g (4oz) Stork® block, plus extra for brushing

200g (7oz) gluten-free self-raising flour

⅛ tsp xanthan gum

150g (5oz) caster sugar

2 egg yolks plus 3 egg whites

4 tbsp raspberry jam

120g (4½oz) desiccated coconut

1. Preheat the oven to 180°C/350°F/Gas Mark 4. Brush a deep baking tin (about 28 x 18 x 4cm/11 x 7 x 1½ inches) with melted Stork® and line the bottom and sides with non-stick baking paper.
2. Put the flour and xanthan gum in a large bowl and rub in the Stork® until the mixture resembles breadcrumbs.
3. Stir in 50g (2oz) of the sugar, then mix in the egg yolks and gather into a soft dough. Press evenly into the bottom of the prepared tin and spread the jam on top.
4. In a clean bowl, whisk the egg whites to soft peaks. Using a large metal spoon, fold in the remaining sugar and the coconut. Spread over the jam.
5. Bake for 20 minutes, or until the topping is golden. Cool in the tin, then cut into 16 squares.

Note: This cake will keep for up to a week if stored in an airtight container. It can also be frozen, but the base may not be as crisp when defrosted.

OPINEL
INOX

Vegan Banana, Date and Apricot Bars

What could be simpler and tastier than these healthy fruit bars? Just pop everything in a food processor, pack it into a tin and bake.

MAKES 12

120g (4½oz) Stork® block, plus extra for brushing

150g (5oz) pitted dates

75g (3oz) dried apricots

25g (1oz) raisins

2 ripe bananas, peeled

200g (7oz) porridge oats

60g (2¼oz) plain wholemeal flour

2 tbsp soya or almond milk

3 tbsp maple syrup

3 tbsp mixed seeds

1 tsp ground cinnamon

1. Preheat the oven to 180°C/350°F/Gas Mark 4. Brush a 20cm (8 inch) square cake tin with melted Stork® and line it with non-stick baking paper.
2. Place all the ingredients in a food processor and blend to a crumbly paste.
3. Tip the mixture into the prepared tin and use the back of a wooden spoon to press it down firmly.
4. Bake for 20–25 minutes, until pale golden. Leave to cool in the tin, then cut into 12 squares.

4

Biscuits and Cookies

Peanut and Raisin Cookies

It takes just minutes to rustle up a batch of these scrummy cookies, and minutes to eat them all too.

MAKES 20

100g (4oz) Stork® spread, plus extra for brushing

225g (8oz) soft light brown sugar

1 egg

1 tsp vanilla extract

100g (4oz) wholemeal flour

100g (4oz) self-raising flour

100g (4oz) peanut and raisin mix

1. Preheat the oven to 190°C/375°F/Gas Mark 5. Brush two non-stick baking sheets with melted Stork®.
2. Place all the ingredients in a bowl and mix until blended (1–2 minutes).
3. Using a dessertspoon, place spoonfuls of the mixture on the prepared baking sheets. Flatten slightly, then bake for 8–10 minutes.
4. Transfer to a wire rack to cool slightly, and eat while still warm.

VARIATION

Replace the peanut and raisin mix with 75g (3oz) chocolate chips and 25g (1oz) chopped walnuts.

Viennese Whirls

These delicate biscuits can be piped as swirls or, if you prefer, into finger shapes. In both cases, try dipping the ends in melted chocolate before sandwiching with buttercream.

MAKES 10

250g (9oz) Stork® spread

50g (2oz) icing sugar, plus extra for dusting

2 tbsp cornflour

250g (9oz) plain flour

½ tsp vanilla extract

2 tbsp raspberry jam

FOR THE ICING

50g (2oz) Stork® spread

120g (4½oz) icing sugar, sifted

½ tsp vanilla extract

1. Preheat the oven to 190°C/375°F/Gas Mark 5. Line two baking trays with non-stick baking paper.
2. Put the Stork® and sugar in a bowl and beat until very creamy.
3. Sift in the cornflour and flour, add the vanilla and beat well to form a soft dough.
4. Place the mixture in a piping bag fitted with a large star nozzle and pipe 20 swirls on the prepared trays. Bake for 13–15 minutes, until golden with slightly browned edges. Leave to cool completely on the baking trays.
5. To make the icing, beat the Stork®, sugar and vanilla together in a bowl until soft and creamy.
6. Spread half the biscuits with a little icing and place ½ teaspoon jam in the centre of each. Top with a second biscuit and dust with icing sugar.

Note: These biscuits will keep for up to a week in an airtight container.

The title of this 1963 Stork® booklet alludes to a popular television programme in which guests were set tasks to complete in one minute or less. Here, of course, the idea was to produce delicious food in record time.

BEAT THE CLOCK WITH STORK
FROM THE STORK COOKERY SERVICE

Shortbread Fingers

There's nothing more welcoming than offering friends a piece of shortbread when they come to visit, so make sure to have some in the cake tin at all times.

MAKES 12

225g (8oz) Stork® block, plus extra for brushing

100g (4oz) caster sugar, plus extra for dusting

300g (11 oz) plain flour, plus extra for dusting

100g (4oz) ground rice

1. Preheat the oven to 160°C/325°F/Gas Mark 3. Brush a 28 x 18cm (11 x 7 inch) Swiss roll tin with melted Stork® and dust with flour.
2. Put the Stork® and sugar into a food processor and whizz until softened. Add the flour and ground rice and pulse until the mixture resembles fine breadcrumbs. (This step can be done by hand if you prefer.)
3. Using the back of a wooden spoon, press the mixture into the prepared tin and smooth the surface.
4. Using a sharp knife, mark out 12 fingers and prick the surface with a fork. Dust with extra caster sugar and bake for about 40 minutes.
5. Cool in the tin for 5 minutes before turning out. Carefully break along the lines into 12 fingers.

VARIATION

Lemon or orange shortbread: Add the grated zest of a small lemon or orange to the basic recipe.

Although this advertisement has a distinctly 1930s' feel, it was actually produced in 1982. Its aim was to lure people away from shop-bought cakes and back to home baking.

Bake them a slice of yesterday.
Stork
IT'S ONLY PROPER

Bourbon Biscuits

These biscuits are perennial favourites that give a double hit of chocolate. Fill them with vanilla icing if you prefer – just omit the cocoa powder and increase the icing sugar instead.

MAKES 15

120g (4½oz) plain flour, plus extra for dusting

25g (1oz) cocoa powder

65g (2½oz) Stork® block

50g (2oz) light muscovado sugar

2 tbsp golden syrup

1 tbsp milk

FOR THE FILLING

50g (2oz) Stork® spread

75g (3oz) icing sugar

1 tbsp cocoa powder

1 tsp vanilla extract

Splash of milk, if needed

1. Place the flour and cocoa powder in a bowl. Add the Stork® and rub in until the mixture resembles breadcrumbs.
2. Using a wooden spoon, stir in the sugar and golden syrup until the mixture begins to clump together. Add the milk, mixing to make a soft dough and bringing it together with your hands.
3. Turn out the dough, wrap it in clingfilm and chill for 20 minutes.
4. Preheat the oven to 180°C/350°F/Gas Mark 4. Line two baking sheets with non-stick baking paper.
5. Lightly flour a work surface and roll the chilled dough into a 15 x 10cm (6 x 4 inch) rectangle about 3mm (⅛ inch) thick. Using a ruler to help you, cut the dough in half lengthways, then cut each strip into 15 rectangles 5cm (2 inches) long and 3cm (1¼ inches) wide. Transfer to the prepared baking sheets and prick with a fork.
6. Bake for 12–13 minutes, or until the biscuits are firm and dry. Leave to cool on the sheets for 10 minutes, then transfer to a wire rack to cool completely.
7. To make the filling, put the Stork®, icing sugar, cocoa powder and vanilla in a bowl and beat until smooth and creamy. If necessary to get the right consistency, add the milk, a spoonful at a time.
8. Spread half the biscuits with the filling (a heaped teaspoon on each), then sandwich together with the remaining biscuits.

The Stork® Demonstration Van visited agricultural shows all around the country with the aim of introducing people to lots of new and interesting recipes. This booklet contained a selection of them.

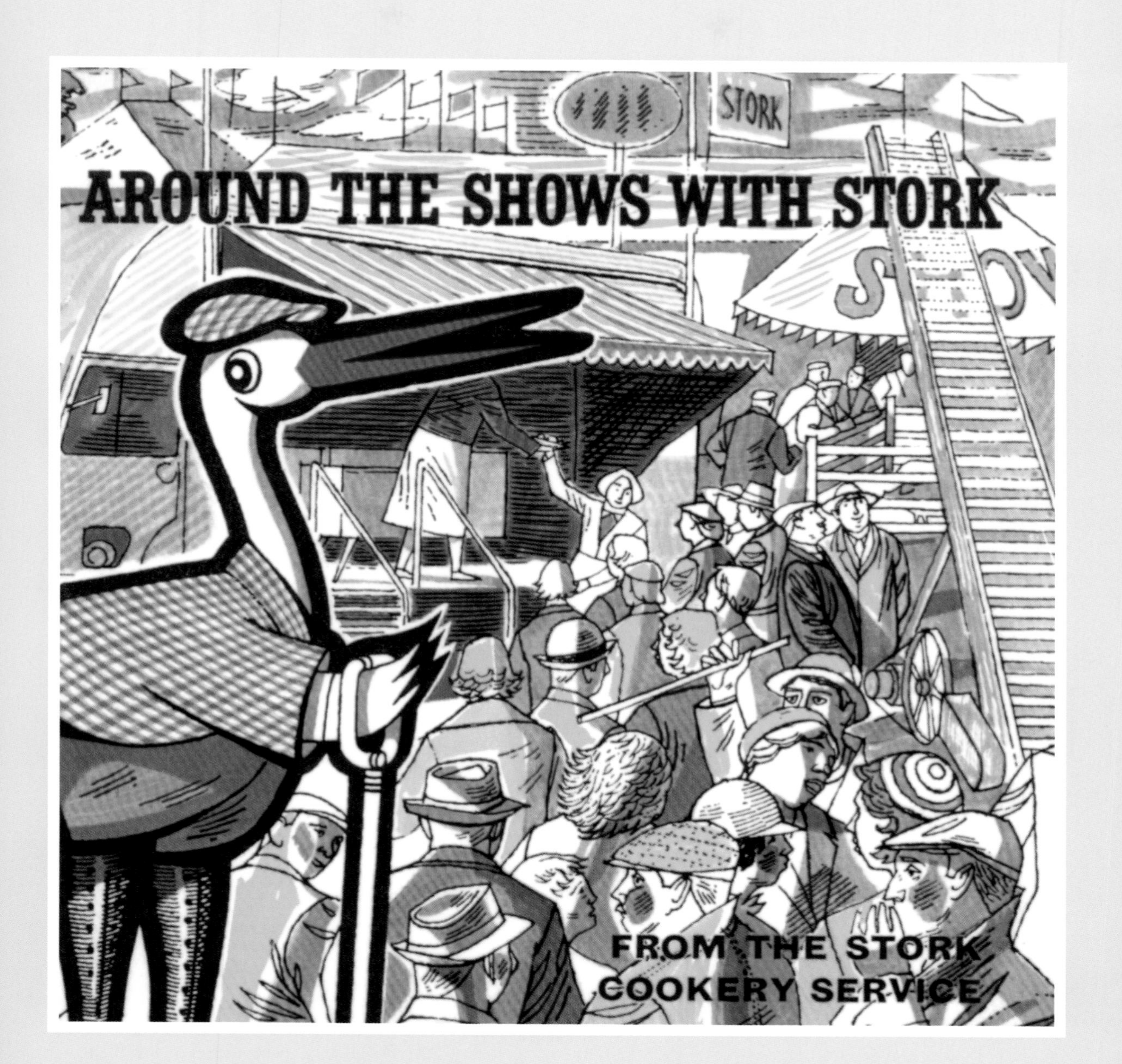
STORK
AROUND THE SHOWS WITH STORK
FROM THE STORK
COOKERY SERVICE

Chocolate Crackle Cookies

The crazy paving effect of these cookies is made by rolling the dough in icing sugar before baking; as it rises, the sugary crust reveals the soft chocolate interior beneath. So scrummy!

MAKES 18–20

175g (6oz) dark chocolate (60% cocoa solids)

4 tbsp Stork® spread

2 eggs, beaten

150g (5oz) caster sugar

175g (6oz) plain flour

½ tsp baking powder

1 tsp vanilla extract

40g (1½oz) icing sugar, plus extra for dusting

1. Preheat the oven to 325°F/160°C/Gas Mark 3. Line two baking sheets with non-stick baking paper.
2. Melt the chocolate in a small bowl set over a pan of simmering water, then stir in the Stork® until smooth. Leave to cool for 5 minutes.
3. Whisk the eggs and caster sugar together in a bowl until pale, then whisk in the chocolate mixture.
4. Stir in the flour, baking powder and vanilla, and mix to a soft dough. Cover and chill for at least 2 hours.
5. Break the chilled dough into golf ball-sized pieces and roll them into balls.
6. Roll each ball thickly in the icing sugar, then place on the prepared baking sheets, spacing them well apart. Flatten with your fingers until they are about 1cm (½ inch) thick. Sprinkle with a little more icing sugar.
7. Bake for 12–13 minutes, until the edges are crisp but the centre is still slightly soft. Allow to cool on the baking sheet for 10 minutes before transferring to a wire rack to cool completely.

Although produced in the 1970s, the style of this recipe booklet harks back to an earlier time, when home-baked biscuits and buns were part of every picnic.

Memories are made of this
NEW
Stork
Seven traditional recipes from Stork.

Gluten-free Lime and Raspberry Jammy Dodgers

Unlike many gluten-free biscuits, which can be a bit dry and crumbly, these are crisp and packed with a lovely jammy centre. They're bound to make the whole family smile.

Gf

MAKES 16

200g (7oz) Stork® block

100g (4oz) caster sugar

300g (11oz) gluten-free plain flour

Pinch of fine sea salt

1 tsp vanilla extract

2 tbsp lime juice

FOR THE FILLING

75g (3oz) Stork® block

120g (4½oz) icing sugar, plus extra for dusting

1 tsp lime juice

4 tbsp raspberry jam

1. Cream the Stork® and sugar in a bowl for about 5 minutes, until pale and fluffy. Add the flour, salt, vanilla and lime juice and mix just until it comes together as a stiff dough.
2. Turn the dough onto a work surface and shape into a ball. Wrap in clingfilm and chill for 10 minutes.
3. Preheat the oven to 180°C/350°F/Gas Mark 4. Line two baking sheets with non-stick baking paper.
4. Roll out the chilled dough to the thickness of a £1 coin, then use a 6cm (2½ inch) cutter to stamp out 16 circles. Using a 3cm (1¼ inch) cutter, stamp out a hole in the centre of each circle. Lay the holed circles on a prepared baking sheet. Reroll the dough trimmings and cut out another 16 circles, but don't stamp out any holes this time. Lay these circles on the second baking sheet.
5. Bake both sheets of biscuits for 12 minutes, until pale golden at the edges. Transfer to a wire rack and allow to cool completely.
6. To make the buttercream filling, beat the Stork® and icing sugar with the lime juice until smooth and creamy, then spoon into a piping bag and snip off the end.
7. Pipe a ring of buttercream on each whole biscuit just inside the edge. Fill the centre with a little jam and place a holed biscuit on top. Dust with icing sugar and serve.

Vegan Oat and Cranberry Cookies

Chewy, packed with oats and fruit, and very, very tasty, these cookies will be enjoyed by everyone.

MAKES 16

100g (4oz) porridge oats

75g (3oz) desiccated coconut

100g (4oz) plain flour

100g (4oz) light muscovado sugar

50g (2oz) dried cranberries

Pinch of ground mixed spice

100g (4oz) Stork® block

1 tbsp golden syrup

2 tbsp water

1 tsp bicarbonate of soda

1. Preheat the oven to 180°C/350°F/Gas Mark 4. Line two baking sheets with non-stick baking paper.
2. Put the oats, coconut, flour, sugar, cranberries and mixed spice in a bowl.
3. Place the Stork®, golden syrup and water in a small pan and heat until the Stork® has melted.
4. Add the bicarbonate of soda to the pan and, as soon as it froths up, pour it into the bowl of dry ingredients, stirring gently to make a soft dough.
5. Place heaped teaspoonfuls of the mixture on the baking sheets, spacing them about 2.5cm (1 inch) apart to allow room for expansion.
6. Flatten the mounds slightly with a knife and bake for 8–10 minutes, until golden brown.
7. Allow to cool and harden on the baking tray for 10 minutes, before cooling on a wire rack.

The front cover of this booklet, dating from the 1960s, shows how horizons had broadened and people were taking more adventurous holidays. Of course, Stork® was a store-cupboard essential whatever the location.

Away from it all
with STORK
FROM THE STORK COOKERY SERVICE

Vegan Florentines

Sometimes it's nice to serve something rather elegant and dainty, and these fit the bill. They look posh but are so simple to make. Serve with coffee or alongside a light dessert.

MAKES 20

50g (2oz) Stork® block
50g (2oz) caster sugar
50g (2oz) golden syrup
50g (2oz) plain flour
50g (2oz) flaked almonds
50g (2oz) chopped mixed peel
25g (1oz) raisins
50g (2oz) glacé cherries or dried apricots, chopped
150g (5oz) dark chocolate

1. Preheat the oven to 180°C/350°F/Gas Mark 4. Brush three baking trays with melted Stork® and line with non-stick baking paper.
2. Heat the Stork®, sugar and syrup together in a small pan until the sugar dissolves.
3. Stir in the flour, almonds, peel and dried fruit.
4. Place heaped teaspoons of the mixture on the baking trays, spacing them well apart. Flatten slightly with a knife, then bake for 10 minutes, until golden brown.
5. Allow the florentines to cool on the trays for about 10 minutes before transferring them to a wire rack to cool completely.
6. Melt the chocolate in a bowl set over a pan of simmering water.
7. Turn the biscuits upside-down on the wire rack, then spread the chocolate over them, using a fork to make ripples. Leave to set.

Note: The florentines will keep for 2–3 days in an airtight container.

5
Tarts and Pies

Lemon Meringue Pie

Sweet and sharp, this dessert is always a firm family favourite and worth the little effort it takes to make.

SERVES 6

Plain flour, for dusting

1 quantity All-in-one Shortcrust Pastry (see page 138)

25g (1oz) Stork® spread

3 tbsp cornflour

Zest and juice of 1 large lemon

300ml (10fl oz) water

50g (2oz) sugar

2 egg yolks

Glâcé cherries and angelica, to decorate (optional)

FOR THE MERINGUE

2 egg whites

75g (3oz) caster sugar

1. Preheat the oven to 200°C/400°F/Gas Mark 6. Place a 20cm (8 inch) flan dish on a baking sheet and set aside.
2. Lightly flour a work surface, roll out the pastry and use to line the flan dish. Trim off the surplus, then line the pastry case with non-stick baking paper and baking beans and bake for about 10 minutes. Remove the paper and beans, then bake the case for a further 10 minutes, until the pastry is golden. Set aside to cool.
3. To make the filling, place the Stork®, cornflour, lemon zest and juice in a saucepan with the water and sugar and bring to the boil, stirring constantly over a medium heat. Continue boiling and stirring for 2–3 minutes, until thickened and smooth. Cool slightly, then beat in the egg yolks. Pour the mixture into the cooled flan case.
4. To make the meringue, whisk the egg whites into stiff peaks. Carefully fold in the sugar, then pile or pipe the meringue over the filling. Decorate with glacé cherries and angelica, if liked.
5. Bake for 10–15 minutes and serve hot or cold.

Bakewell Tart

Originally featured in Stork's Tour of Britain's Cooking, *produced by the Stork® Cookery Service in 1950, this classic British tart is filled with jam and an almond frangipane, and is always popular. To make it even more special, drizzle with glacé icing once the tart is cold, and top with a glacé cherry too.*

SERVES 6

2 rounded tbsp jam

175g (6oz) ground almonds

100g (4oz) caster sugar

2 eggs, lightly beaten

50g (2oz) Stork® spread

1 tsp almond extract

FOR THE SWEET SHORTCRUST PASTRY

100g (4oz) plain flour, plus extra for dusting

Pinch of salt

65g (2½oz) Stork® spread

15g (½oz) caster sugar

3 tsp water

1. Preheat the oven to 160°C/325°F/Gas Mark 3. Place a 20cm (8 inch) flan dish on a baking sheet and set aside.
2. To make the pastry, sift the flour and salt together into a bowl. Add the Stork® and rub in until the mixture resembles fine breadcrumbs. Stir in the sugar, then add the water and mix with a knife to a firm dough. Using your hands, form it into a ball.
3. Place the dough on a lightly floured work surface and roll out very thinly into a circle about 25cm (10 inches) wide.
4. Lift the pastry onto the rolling pin and use to line the flan dish. Trim off the surplus, then spread the jam in the bottom of the pastry case.
5. Combine the almonds and sugar in a bowl, stir in the eggs, then beat well.
6. Melt the Stork®, add to the egg mixture along with the almond extract and stir well. Pour into the flan case and spread evenly.
7. Bake for 70–75 minutes, until it is springy to the touch, and serve either hot or cold.

Around 1958 Stork® provided an opportunity for home cooks to sample some regional specialities from various parts of the British Isles. This booklet focused on the traditional with a modern twist.

STORK'S TOUR
of Britain's cooking
STORK
FROM THE STORK COOKERY SERVICE

Profiteroles

Light as air, filled with luscious whipped cream and topped with chocolate icing, profiteroles are probably everyone's favourite dessert.

SERVES 4

150ml (5fl oz) whipping cream

FOR THE CHOUX PASTRY

300ml (10fl oz) water

100g (4oz) Stork® spread

150g (5oz) plain flour, sifted

Pinch of salt

½ tsp vanilla extract

4 eggs

FOR THE CHOCOLATE SAUCE

50g (2oz) dark chocolate, broken into pieces

4 tbsp golden syrup

15g (½oz) Stork® spread

1. Preheat the oven to 220°C/425°F/Gas Mark 7. Set out a baking sheet.
2. To make the pastry, put the water and Stork® into a small saucepan and bring to the boil.
3. Add the sifted flour and salt, stirring vigorously until a ball forms. Cool slightly, then add the vanilla.
4. Beat in the eggs one at a time, and continue beating until the paste is perfectly smooth.
5. Dampen the baking sheet and place teaspoons of the choux mixture on it, spacing them well apart. Bake for 15 minutes, then lower the temperature to 190°C/375°F/Gas Mark 5 and bake for a further 15–20 minutes, until golden brown and well risen.
6. Transfer the choux buns to a wire rack, make a slit in the side of each one and leave until cold.
7. To make the chocolate sauce, place all the ingredients for it in a small heatproof bowl set over a pan of simmering water and leave to melt. Beat until smooth and glossy.
8. Whip the cream and spoon it into a piping bag fitted with a plain nozzle. Stick the nozzle into the slit in each bun and fill with the whipped cream.
9. Arrange the profiteroles in a pyramid on a plate and drizzle with the chocolate sauce before serving.

Eclairs

Why not rustle up a batch of these elegant pastries one Sunday afternoon as a treat for the family? They really don't take long to make, and everyone will love you for it.

MAKES 10–12

Stork® spread, for brushing

1 quantity Choux Pastry (see page 132)

150ml (5fl oz) double cream

1 quantity Glacé Icing (see page 158), flavoured as you like

1. Preheat the oven to 220°C/425°F/Gas Mark 7. Brush two baking sheets with melted Stork®.
2. Spoon the pastry into a piping bag fitted with a large plain nozzle and pipe 7.5cm (3 inch) strips onto the baking sheets, spacing them well apart.
3. Bake for 15 minutes, then swap the sheets around, lower the temperature to 190°C/375°F/Gas Mark 5 and bake for a further 20–25 minutes.
4. Transfer to a wire rack, make a slit in the side of each pastry, then leave until cold.
5. Whip the cream and spoon it into a piping bag fitted with a plain nozzle. Stick the nozzle into the slit in each pastry and fill with the whipped cream.
6. Using a palette knife dipped in hot water, spread your chosen icing on top of each éclair and leave to set.

   Note: If you want to freeze the éclairs, do so before filling and decorating them. Defrost thoroughly before following steps 5 and 6.

The front cover of this 1960s recipe booklet was designed to appeal to an increasingly sophisticated audience who holidayed abroad and wanted to re-create foreign dishes at home.

STORK GOES CONTINENTAL

FROM THE

COOKERY SERVICE

Custard Tart

A comforting, old-fashioned and fabulous treat: it's the nutmeg on top of this tart that really finishes it off and gives a real hit of flavour.

SERVES 4–6

1 baked sweet shortcrust pastry case (see page 130)

FOR THE FILLING

2 eggs

2 tbsp caster sugar

300ml (10fl oz) milk

Pinch of ground nutmeg

1. Preheat the oven to 190°C/375°F/Gas Mark 5.
2. To make the custard filling, beat the eggs and sugar together in a bowl.
3. Heat the milk in a pan until almost boiling, then pour it over the beaten eggs, stirring well. Cool and strain into a jug.
4. Carefully pour the custard mixture into the pastry case and sprinkle with nutmeg.
5. Bake for 25–35 minutes, or until the custard has set.

Apple Pie

If you want to dish up a big slice of love, make this apple pie and serve it with a big jug of hot custard – everyone will thank you for it.

SERVES 4–6

750g (1½lb) cooking apples

75g (3oz) sugar

2 tbsp water

6 cloves (optional)

Flour, for dusting

1 quantity all-in-one shortcrust pastry (see page 138)

Caster sugar, for sprinkling

1. Preheat the oven to 200°C/400°F/Gas Mark 6. Set out a 900ml (1½ pint) pie dish and place a pie funnel or upturned egg cup in the centre.
2. Peel, core and slice the apples. Layer them in the pie dish around the funnel, sprinkling each layer with the sugar, measured water and cloves (if using), finishing with a layer of fruit.
3. Lightly flour a work surface and roll out the pastry to a thickness of 5mm (¼ inch), making sure it is at least 2.5cm (1 inch) larger all round than the pie dish.
4. Cut off narrow strips around the edge of the pastry and use extra water to stick them around the rim of the pie dish. Press them down gently and brush with more water.
5. Lift the remaining pastry onto the rolling pin and use it to cover the dish, pressing gently onto the strips around the rim. Trim off the surplus pastry, then flute the edge and make a hole in the centre for steam to escape.
6. Brush the pastry with water and sprinkle with caster sugar before baking for 30–40 minutes. Serve hot or cold.

Note: The pie can be frozen before or after baking.

VARIATIONS

Blackberry and apple pie: Omit the cloves and use 225g (8oz) blackberries and 450g (1lb) cooking apples.

Plum, rhubarb, gooseberry or blackcurrant pie: Omit the cloves, sugar and water, and use a large can of your chosen fruit, including just enough juice from it to come three-quarters of the way up the pie dish.

Lemon Curd Tart

The pastry used here is simplicity itself to make, and the lemon curd filling is light and deliciously tangy. For this classic recipe you need a traditional pie plate.

SERVES 4–6

175g (6oz) lemon curd

Grated zest of 1 lemon

75g (3oz) fresh breadcrumbs

FOR THE ALL-IN-ONE SHORTCRUST PASTRY

225g (8oz) Stork® spread

3 tbsp water

350g (12oz) plain flour, plus extra for dusting

1. Preheat the oven to 200°C/400°F/Gas Mark 6. Set out an ungreased 23cm (9 inch) pie plate.
2. To make the pastry, place the Stork®, water and one-third of the flour in a bowl and cream with a fork until well mixed (1–2 minutes). Stir in the remaining flour to form a firm dough.
3. Turn the dough onto a lightly floured work surface and knead thoroughly until smooth and silky.
4. Roll out the pastry to the thickness of a 10p coin and use to line the pie plate. Press down gently, then trim off the excess and flute around the edge.
5. Using a spoon dipped into hot water, measure the lemon curd into a bowl. Add the lemon zest and breadcrumbs and mix well. Spread this mixture over the pastry, leaving a clear 1cm (½ inch) border around the edge.
6. Reroll the pastry trimmings and cut into long, narrow strips. Use the strips to make a lattice over the filling, dampening the ends to stick them down.
7. Bake for 30–35 minutes.

For generations, housewives were judged on the quality of the pastry they produced and praised for having a 'light hand'. However, this 1930s booklet proved that there was no secret to producing excellent pastry, apart from using Stork®.

ALL ABOUT

PASTRY

BY THE

STORK COOKERY SERVICE

Free-form Plum Tart

This is a lovely rustic dessert, and you can fill the pastry case with any seasonal fruit: try apricots or apples and blackberries, and serve with plenty of clotted cream.

MAKES 4 X 15CM (6 INCH) TARTS OR A 20CM (8 INCH) TART THAT WILL SERVE 6

200g (7oz) plain flour, plus extra for dusting

Pinch of salt

100g (4oz) Stork® block, cubed

½ tsp ground cinnamon

2 tbsp granulated sugar, plus extra for sprinkling

4 tbsp cold water

8 ripe plums, halved and stoned

50g (2oz) walnuts, chopped

Grated zest of ½ orange

1 egg white

1. Preheat the oven to 220°C/425°F/Gas Mark 7. Set out a non-stick baking tray.
2. Place the flour and salt in a bowl, add the Stork® and rub in until the mixture resembles breadcrumbs.
3. Stir in the cinnamon and half the sugar. Add 3 tablespoons of the water and mix to a soft dough.
4. Turn the dough onto a well-floured work surface and shape into a ball. Roll out thinly into a circle about 30cm (12 inches) in diameter, or cut into 4 equal pieces and roll each one into a circle 15cm (6 inches) in diameter.
5. Cut each plum half into 3 lengthways slices. Place in a bowl and toss with the remaining sugar, the walnuts and orange zest.
6. Pile the plums into the centre of the pastry circle(s). Gather about 2cm (¾ inch) of the pastry edge and bring it up around the plums, pinching it at intervals to make a rim. Brush all the exposed pastry with egg white and sprinkle with a little extra sugar.
7. Bake for 15 minutes, or until the pastry is golden brown and crisp. Serve warm with custard or cream.

Cookery myths. Old wives' tales

Exploring the myths in basic cookery.

Proof about the pudding. A guide to storing foods. Historic preserving.

Kitchen facts and fables. Fun food quiz.

Stork Cookery Service

Apple and Blackberry Turnovers

It might seem like a palaver to make rough puff pastry, but it's actually quite easy, and when you taste these flaky, fruit-filled treats, you will realise the effort was worth it.

MAKES 6

2 small Bramley cooking apples

4 tbsp caster sugar

Juice of 1 small lemon

2 tbsp cornflour

200g (7oz) blackberries

1 egg, beaten

2 tbsp icing sugar, for dusting

FOR THE ROUGH PUFF PASTRY

1 x 250g (9oz) Stork® block, frozen, plus 175g (6oz), chilled

300g (11 oz) plain flour, plus extra for dusting

Pinch of salt

6–8 tbsp water

1. Peel, core and dice the apples. Place in a pan with the sugar and 1 tablespoon of the lemon juice, then cover and cook for 5 minutes, until some apples are puréed while some are still chunky and firm.

2. Mix the cornflour with 1 tablespoon of the lemon juice, add to the apples and cook until thickened. Transfer the mixture to a shallow bowl. When cool, stir in the blackberries.

3. To make the pastry, cut 50g (2oz) off the frozen Stork®, cut into cubes and set aside. Return the remainder of the frozen block to the freezer. Mix the flour and salt together in a bowl. Rub in the cubed Stork®, then gradually mix in enough of the water to form a soft dough.

4. Lightly flour a work surface and roll the dough into a 30 x 12cm (12 x 5 inch) rectangle. With the short edge nearest you, grate half the frozen Stork® over the bottom two-thirds of the dough. Fold down the top third and fold up the bottom third. Turn the dough 90 degrees and roll it again into a 30 x 12cm (12 x 5 inch) rectangle.

5. Again with the short edge nearest you, grate the remaining frozen Stork® over the bottom two-thirds of the dough. Fold and turn once more, as in step 5, then wrap the dough in clingfilm and freeze for 15 minutes. Remove from the freezer and refrigerate for 15 minutes.

6. Preheat the oven to 220°C/450°F/Gas Mark 7. Flour a work surface and roll the dough into a 38 x 25cm (15 x 10 inch) rectangle. Using a sharp knife and a ruler, cut out six 12 x 12cm (5 x 5 inch) pastry squares.

7. Spoon the apple filling equally into the centre of the squares. Brush beaten egg around two adjacent sides of each square, then fold the unbrushed pastry over to make triangles, pressing the edges to seal. Crimp the edges with a fork and pierce the top to allow steam to escape.

8. Place the pastries on a baking sheet and brush with beaten egg. Bake for 15–20 minutes, until dark golden brown. Dust with icing sugar and serve warm or cold.

Minted Pea and Bacon Quiche

This is the perfect quiche to serve for a summer buffet spread or lunch with friends. It's packed with flavour from the peas and mint, so you can omit the bacon if serving it to vegetarians.

SERVES 8

15g (½oz) Stork® block

2 shallots, peeled and finely diced

75g (3oz) smoked streaky bacon rashers, snipped into strips

225g (8oz) frozen peas

3 eggs

300ml (10fl oz) crème fraîche

10g (¼oz) mint leaves, finely chopped

50g (2oz) Parmesan cheese, grated

¼ tsp salt

¼ tsp freshly ground black pepper

FOR THE PASTRY

225g (8oz) plain flour, plus extra for dusting

Pinch of salt

120g (4½oz) Stork® block, cubed

25g (1oz) Parmesan cheese, finely grated

2 tbsp cold water

1. Set out a 23cm (9 inch) loose-bottomed flan tin.
2. To make the pastry, sift the flour and salt together into a bowl. Add the Stork® and rub in until the mixture resembles fine breadcrumbs. Stir in the Parmesan, then add the water and mix with a knife to form a firm dough. Using your hands, shape it into a ball.
3. Roll out the pastry on a lightly floured work surface to the thickness of a £1 coin and use to line the flan tin. Chill for 10 minutes.
4. Preheat the oven to 200°C/400°F/Gas Mark 6.
5. Line the pastry case with a circle of non-stick baking paper and fill with baking beans. Blind bake for 15 minutes, then remove the paper and beans and bake for a further 5–10 minutes, until the pastry is crisp and dry. Set aside and reduce the oven temperature to 190°C/375°F/Gas Mark 5.
6. To make the filling, melt the Stork® in a small frying pan and fry the shallots and bacon over a medium heat for 10 minutes, until the shallots have softened.
7. Meanwhile, place the peas in a bowl, cover with boiling water and leave to defrost for 5 minutes. Drain and pat dry.
8. Beat the eggs and crème fraîche together, then stir in the shallots, bacon, peas, mint and Parmesan. Add the seasoning and pour the mixture into the pastry case. Bake for 30 minutes, until golden brown and set. Serve at room temperature or cold.

Designed to help the busy housewife who also held down a job outside the home, this 1959 booklet offered 'a wide selection of supper-time savouries' that were quick, easy to prepare and very appetising.

Savoury suppers
WITH Stork
from the Stork Cookery Service

Pork, Sweet Potato and Chorizo Pies

Everyone loves a pie, and these tasty handfuls are simple to make and packed with meat and veg – a complete meal in one. Delicious served hot or cold with salad.

MAKES 8

500g (1lb 2oz) minced pork

1 onion, finely chopped

100g (4oz) chorizo, diced

350g (12oz) sweet potato, peeled and diced

1 tsp harissa paste

½ tsp dried mixed herbs

6 tbsp tomato passata

Salt and freshly ground black pepper

1 egg, beaten, to glaze

FOR THE PASTRY

400g (14oz) plain flour, plus extra for dusting

1 tsp salt

200g (7oz) Stork® block, cubed

6–8 tbsp cold water

1. Dry-fry the minced pork with the onion and chorizo for about 5 minutes, until browned and the onions are beginning to soften. Add the sweet potato, season with plenty of salt and pepper, then add the harissa and herbs. Stir in the passata, cover and simmer for 10 minutes. Transfer to a plate to cool rapidly while you make the pastry.

2. Place the flour and salt in a bowl, add the Stork® and rub it in until the mixture resembles fine breadcrumbs. Mix in enough of the water to form a dough. Roll into a ball, wrap in clingfilm and chill for 30 minutes.

3. Preheat the oven to 200°C/400°F/Gas Mark 6. Place eight 10cm (4 inch) fluted flan tins on a baking tray.

4. Place the chilled pastry on a floured work surface, cut off one-third and reserve for the lids. Cut the remaining pastry into 8 equal pieces and roll each into a circle large enough to line the individual flan tins. Take care to press the pastry against the sides, easing it smoothly into the flutes, but leaving the top edge a bit uneven.

5. Spoon the pork mixture equally into the pastry cases. Reroll the pastry trimmings with the reserved pastry and cut out eight 10cm (4 inch) circles. Dampen the edge of the pastry in the tins with a little water, then place the lids on top, pressing the edges together.

6. Brush the pies with the beaten egg and bake for 35 minutes, until golden brown and crisp. Serve hot or cold.

Vegan Roasted Vegetable Pizza Tart

The great thing about this pizza-like tart is that it can be topped with any roasted vegetables that are in season. Try courgettes and tomatoes, and add a sprinkling of vegan cheese if you wish.

SERVES 6

300g (11 oz) butternut squash, peeled and cubed

2 small raw beetroot, cubed

2 red peppers, deseeded and quartered

2 tbsp basil-infused olive oil

1 tsp dried thyme

Plain flour, for dusting

1 quantity chilled Rough Puff Pastry (see page 142)

3 tbsp sundried tomato purée

150g (5oz) cherry tomatoes, halved

75g (3oz) sun-soaked tomatoes in oil, drained

50g (2oz) black olives, pitted

Salt and freshly ground black pepper

Basil leaves, to garnish

1. Preheat the oven to 220°C/425°F/Gas Mark 7.
2. Scatter the squash, beetroot and peppers into a large baking tray. Drizzle with the olive oil, season well and sprinkle with the thyme. Roast for 30 minutes, until the vegetables are almost tender.
3. Lightly flour a work surface and roll the pastry into a 35 x 25cm (14 x 10 inch) rectangle. Transfer to a baking sheet, prick all over with a fork, then spread with the tomato purée, leaving a 2.5cm (1 inch) margin around the edge.
4. Scatter the roasted vegetables over the purée, then dot with both lots of the tomatoes and the olives.
5. Bake for 15–18 minutes, or until the pastry has risen and all the vegetables are tender. Garnish with basil leaves and serve immediately.

Vegan Strawberry Apple Tart

This elegant tart would not look out of place on the shelves of a smart patisserie. Added to that, it tastes as good as it looks.

SERVES 8

3 Bramley cooking apples
2 tbsp cold water
2–3 tbsp granulated sugar
350g (12oz) strawberries

FOR THE PASTRY

200g (7oz) self-raising flour, plus extra for dusting
100g (4oz) Stork® block
1 tbsp caster sugar
2 tbsp cold water

FOR THE DRIZZLE

150g (5oz) raspberries
1 tsp icing sugar, or to taste

1. Preheat the oven to 200°C/400°F/Gas Mark 6. Line a deep 20cm (8 inch) loose-bottomed flan tin with non-stick baking paper.
2. To make the pastry, place the flour, Stork® and sugar in a bowl and rub together until the mixture resembles fine breadcrumbs. Add the water and bring the mixture together into a ball. Wrap in clingfilm and chill for 10 minutes.
3. Roll out the pastry on a lightly floured work surface and use to line the prepared flan tin. Chill for 10 minutes.
4. Line the chilled pastry case with non-stick baking paper and baking beans and bake blind for 10 minutes. Remove the paper and beans, reduce the temperature to 190°C/375°F/Gas Mark 5 and bake the pastry case for a further 10 minutes, until golden. Set aside to cool.
5. Meanwhile peel, core and chop the apples and place in a saucepan with the water and granulated sugar. Cover with a lid and cook over a medium heat until the apples have broken down. Continue to cook uncovered, stirring until most of the liquid has evaporated to leave a thick purée. Chill.
6. When the apple purée is cold, pour it into the pastry case and smooth the surface. Top with the strawberries, pointed end upwards.
7. To make the drizzle, use a wooden spoon to push the raspberries through a sieve into a bowl. Sweeten with the icing sugar. Drizzle a little over the tart and offer the remainder separately in a jug.

Stork® continued to produce recipe booklets, such as this one from the late 1950s, long after wartime shortages had ceased. They were always full of interesting and time-saving ideas.

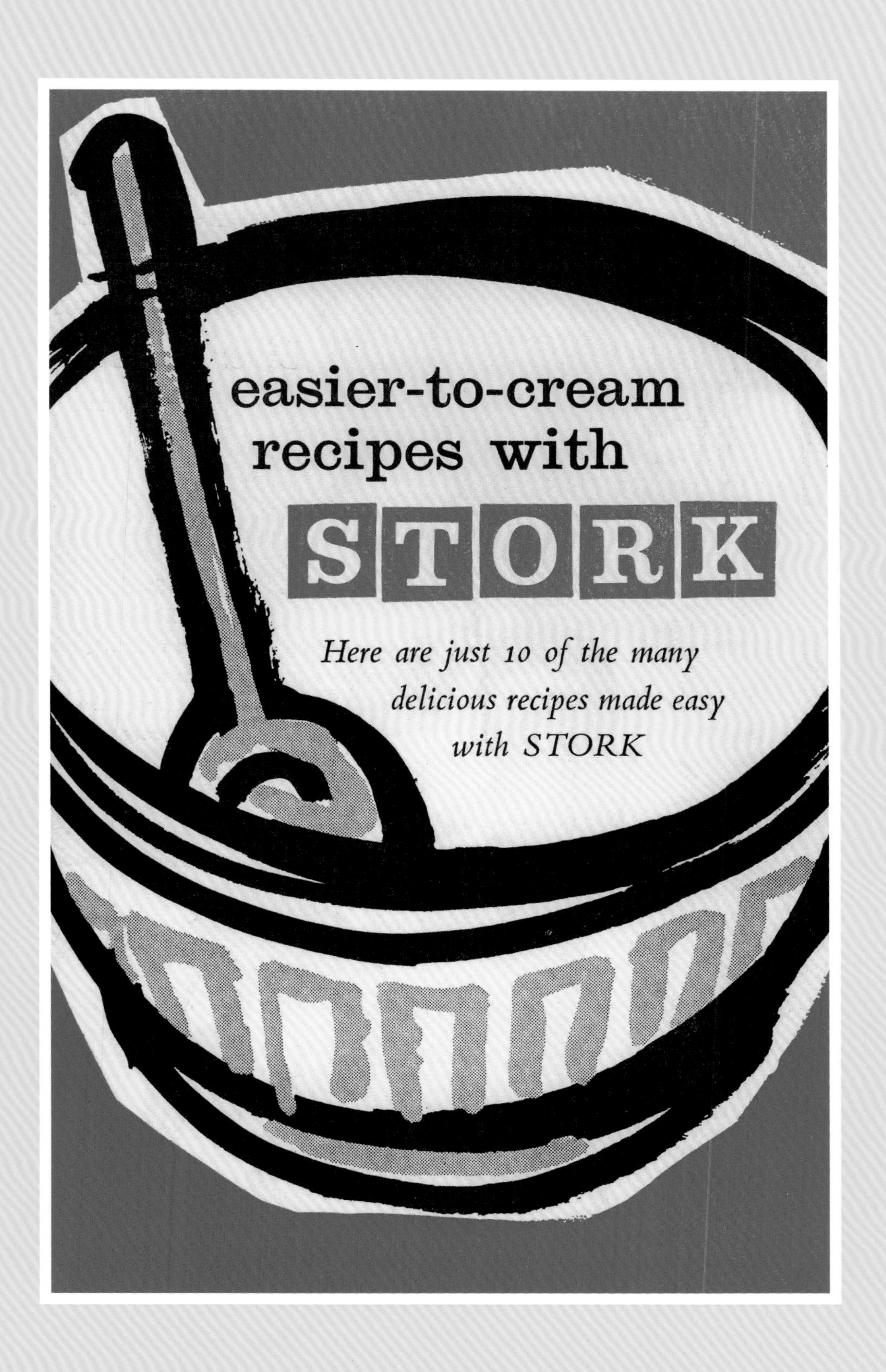
easier-to-cream
recipes with
STORK
Here are just 10 of the many
delicious recipes made easy
with STORK

6
Icings

Stork® Icing

Stork® has been helping people to make better icing since its very first Stork® Cookery Service book was produced in the 1940s. Totally reliable and utterly simple, this recipe should be your go-to icing for every birthday cake. It will take any flavouring you like.

MAKES ENOUGH TO FILL AND ICE A 20CM (8INCH) CAKE

75g (3oz) Stork® spread
225g (8oz) icing sugar, sifted
About 2 tbsp milk, water or fruit juice
Food colouring and flavouring (optional)

1. Beat the Stork® in a bowl until soft and creamy.
2. Add half the sifted icing sugar and beat until light and fluffy.
3. Add the remaining sugar and liquid, and beat thoroughly.
4. If using colouring, add a drop at a time, stirring in each drop before adding the next, until the right shade is obtained. Add any flavouring similarly, tasting for strength after mixing in each drop.
5. Place the cake on an upturned plate. Pour the icing on top, then spread it around with a palette knife. Alternatively, the cake may be sliced in half horizontally, filled with a thin layer of the icing, sandwiched together again, and topped with the remaining icing. If using for small cakes, spread the icing with a teaspoon or table knife, then pattern the surface with a fork if you wish.
6. Add your chosen decorations while the icing is still soft.

A step-by-step guide for beginners to icing, the 1951 booklet opposite reflects the fashion for elaborately iced cakes, a reaction to the austerity of the war years.

VARIATIONS

Chocolate flavour: Omit the colouring and flavouring. Use milk or water to mix the icing. Blend 2 rounded teaspoons (or more, according to taste) sifted cocoa powder, drinking chocolate or grated chocolate with 3 teaspoons boiling water. Cool and beat into the icing.

Coffee flavour: Omit the colouring and flavouring. Use 4 teaspoons milk and 2 teaspoons coffee extract to mix the icing.

Orange or lemon flavour: Omit the colouring and flavouring. Replace with 4 teaspoons orange or lemon juice and just enough water to make a coating consistency.

Peppermint flavour: Use milk or water to mix the icing. Beat in peppermint extract to taste and a tiny amount of green food colouring to make a pale green shade. This flavour goes particularly well with chocolate cakes.

The Art of Icing

Caramel Icing

Rich and sticky, this flavoursome icing transforms an ordinary cake into something special.

MAKES ENOUGH TO COVER AN 18CM (7 INCH) CAKE

1 rounded tbsp golden syrup
25g (1oz) Stork® spread
200g (7oz) sweetened condensed milk
50g (2oz) sugar
½ tsp vanilla extract
Decorations of choice

1. Put the syrup and Stork® in a saucepan and melt over a low heat.
2. Add the condensed milk and sugar. Keeping the heat low, allow the sugar to dissolve completely, occasionally tapping the bottom of the pan with a wooden spoon.
3. When no sugar grains can be felt, bring slowly to the boil, keeping the heat fairly low and stirring constantly. Boil very gently for 15–20 minutes, until a sugar thermometer registers 104–107°C (220–225°F). To test without a thermometer, drop a little of the mixture into a small bowl of cold water. If it can be pressed between the fingers into a soft but firm ball, it is ready. As the mixture is very thick, it should only appear to simmer towards the end, with a slight bubbling all over the surface. Remove from the heat and let the bubbles die down.
4. Add the vanilla, beat well, then cut across the mixture with the spoon or spatula held flat until it thickens and has a curdled appearance. Allow to cool a little.
5. Place the cake to be iced on an upturned plate. Pour the icing onto the middle of it, letting it flow over the sides, then use a palette knife dipped in hot water to spread it where necessary. If preferred, the cake may be sliced in half horizontally, filled with a thin layer of the icing, sandwiched together again, and topped with the remaining icing.
6. Quickly press your chosen decorations into the icing while it is still soft.

To the average housewife in the first half of the twentieth century, 'icing' tended to mean 'royal icing'. As this 1937 Stork® leaflet shows, it created a smooth, hard surface that was ideal for showing off piping skills.

Chocolate Icing

Adding a little Stork® to melted chocolate ensures it is soft enough to cut, rather than shatter, when used to ice a cake.

MAKES ENOUGH TO COVER AND FILL AN 18CM (7 INCH) CAKE

100g (4oz) good-quality dark or milk chocolate

15g (½oz) Stork® spread

1. Break up the chocolate and place in a heatproof bowl with the Stork®.
2. Sit the bowl over a pan of cold water and bring the water to the boil, then reduce the heat to very low and stir the chocolate and Stork® until melted. The temperature of the chocolate should not rise above 43°C (110°F).
3. Remove and cool to about 37°C (98°F) or blood heat. Use as directed for Glacé Icing (see page 158).

Note: Steam or water must not come into direct contact with this type of chocolate icing, or the gloss will be spoilt.

Glacé Icing

This is the icing to choose if you want a glorious shiny coating or elegant drips trailing down the sides of a cake.

MAKES ENOUGH TO COVER AN 18CM (7 INCH) CAKE

100g (4oz) icing sugar

4 tsp warm water

Food colouring and flavouring (optional)

Decorations of choice

1. Sift the icing sugar into a heatproof bowl, then stir in the water.
2. Stand the bowl in a saucepan and pour enough hot water around it to come halfway up the side. Stir over a low heat for 1–2 minutes, or until the sugar has dissolved. Do not allow to become hot.
3. Remove from the heat, cool a little, then stir well and test for consistency. The icing should be thick enough to coat the back of a spoon without running off.
4. If using food colouring, add a drop at a time, stirring in each drop before adding the next, until the right shade is obtained. Add any flavouring similarly, tasting for strength after mixing in each drop.
5. Use a palette knife dipped in hot water to spread the icing over your cake(s) or buns.
6. Quickly press your chosen decorations into the icing while it is still soft.

   Note: Do not touch the top of the cake again until the icing sets, or the gloss will be spoilt.

Satin icing, now known as fondant icing, was a revolution in cake decorating, being ready to roll and easy to shape. In this booklet, Stork® provided great ideas for using it to brighten up cakes and pastries.

GAYER
CAKES
with
SATIN
ICING

Fudge Icing

Smooth and glossy or rough and fudge-like, this is a versatile icing for covering cakes.

MAKES ENOUGH TO COVER A 20CM (8 INCH) CAKE

75g (3oz) Stork® spread
5 tbsp milk
Pinch of salt
450g (1lb) icing sugar
Food colouring and flavouring (optional)

1. Put the Stork®, milk and salt in a saucepan and stir over a fairly low heat until the Stork® has melted. Do not allow to boil – the temperature should not go over 71°C (160°F). Cool a little.
2. Sift the icing sugar into a bowl, pour the Stork® mixture over it and stir well. Leave until almost cold, then beat until thick.
3. If using colouring, add a drop at a time, stirring in each drop before adding the next, until the right shade is obtained. Add any flavouring similarly, tasting for strength after mixing in each drop.
4. Place the cake to be iced on an upturned plate. For a rough finish, spread the icing over the cake with a palette knife, then mark with the tip of the knife or the prongs of a fork. For a glossy finish, pour the icing over when it has been beaten sufficiently to thickly coat the back of a spoon.

VARIATIONS

Chocolate flavour: Increase the milk to 7 tablespoons, and blend 1 rounded and 1 level tablespoon sifted cocoa, drinking chocolate or grated chocolate with the hot mixture before pouring it over the icing sugar.

Coffee flavour: Replace the 5 tablespoons milk with 3 tablespoons milk and 2 tablespoons coffee extract.

Marshmallow Icing

Try spreading this icing on cupcakes or a small sponge for a quick and easy topping.

MAKES ENOUGH TO COVER A 20CM (8 INCH) CAKE

100g (4oz) marshmallows

1–2 drops of food colouring (optional)

1. Place the marshmallows in a heatproof bowl set over a pan of fairly fast-boiling water. Allow to melt, stirring at intervals with a wooden spoon.
2. When the mixture is thick enough to coat the back of the spoon, stir in the food colouring, adding it a drop at a time and mixing well before adding the next, until the right shade is obtained.
3. Place the cake to be iced on an upturned plate. Pour the icing on top, then spread it around with a palette knife.
4. Add your chosen decorations while the icing is still soft.

7 Desserts

Meringues

Here's a classic recipe for all your meringue needs. Use it to make mini meringues sandwiched with cream, meringue nests filled with cream and fruit, or larger decorated meringues that will make stunning centrepieces.

MAKES 12 LARGE OR 24 SMALL MERINGUES

4 egg whites, at room temperature

200g golden or white caster sugar

1. Heat the oven to 150°C/300°F/Gas Mark 2. Line two baking sheets with non-stick baking paper.
2. Put the egg whites in a large, clean bowl and beat them with an electric whisk or mixer at a slow speed until frothy. At that point, increase the speed to medium and whisk until you have a stiff foam that stands upright on the beaters. Don't overbeat or the whites will look fluffy and lumpy.
3. On a high speed, whisk in the sugar a tablespoon at a time and keep whisking until the sugar is fully dissolved and you have a stiff, glossy meringue. This can take up to 10 minutes.
4. Using a metal spoon, place spoonfuls of the meringue on the prepared sheets. The size of the spoon depends on whether you want to make large or small meringues. Don't worry about the shape – just smooth down any spiky bits with a wetted finger. (If you want to make mini pavlovas, use a teaspoon to form each meringue blob into a nest shape.)
5. Place in the oven, lower the heat to 140°C/275°F/Gas Mark 1 and bake for 1 hour. Turn the oven off and leave the meringues in it to cool.

Note: The meringues will keep for several weeks if stored in an airtight container. Add a drop of good colouring in step two for lovely pastel colours.

Wholemeal Lemon Cheesecake

A quick, easy and economical dessert, this can be rustled up in next to no time for family and friends.

Serves 4–6

75g (3oz) wholemeal flour

25g (1oz) ground hazelnuts

50g (2oz) Stork® spread

25g (1oz) caster sugar

For the topping

250g (8oz) low-fat soft cheese

50g (2oz) caster sugar

Grated zest of 1 lemon

100ml (3½fl oz) whipping cream

2 eggs, beaten

Few drops of vanilla extract

For decoration (optional)

Double cream, whipped

Whole hazelnuts

Seasonal fruit (optional)

1. Preheat the oven to 180°C/350°F/Gas Mark 4. Set out a 23cm (9 inch) flan dish.
2. Place all the base ingredients in a bowl and rub in the Stork® until the mixture resembles breadcrumbs. Tip into the prepared dish and press firmly to line the bottom. Bake for 15 minutes.
3. Combine all the topping ingredients in a bowl and beat until smooth. Pour the mixture over the baked base and spread evenly. Bake for 40–45 minutes, until risen and firm.
4. Set aside to cool, then decorate as required, e.g. pipe rosettes of whipped cream around the edge and top with whole hazelnuts, or decorate with seasonal fruit.

Note: The cheesecake can also be made in a microwave. Heat the base on HIGH for 2 minutes. Add the filling, then microwave on LOW for 12 minutes. Set aside to cool.

Key Lime Pie

Dark chocolate and tangy limes make a winning combination, and this impressive American-style dessert will please everyone.

Serves 8

100g (4oz) Stork® spread, plus extra for brushing

300g (11 oz) dark chocolate digestive biscuits

50g (2oz) dark chocolate, plus extra to make 3 tbsp chocolate curls

For the filling

5 limes

1 x 400g (14oz) can condensed milk

300ml (10fl oz) double cream

1. Lightly brush a 20cm (8 inch) loose-bottomed flan tin with melted Stork® and line the bottom with non-stick baking paper.
2. Place the biscuits in a plastic bag and bash with a rolling pin to make fine crumbs.
3. Melt the Stork® and chocolate in a pan over a medium heat, then stir in the biscuit crumbs and heat gently until the mixture is evenly coloured.
4. Tip the biscuit mixture into the prepared tin and use the back of a spoon to press it over the bottom and up the sides. Chill while you make the filling.
5. Using a zester, pare the zest from 1 lime into strips and set aside for decoration. Grate the remaining lime zest and squeeze out all the juice.
6. Place the lime juice in a bowl with the condensed milk and cream and whisk until thickened. Stir in the grated lime zest, then spread this mixture over the biscuit base. Chill for at least 1 hour.
7. Decorate the pie with the reserved strips of zest and the chocolate curls.

Note: The pie will keep for 2–3 days in the fridge, or can be frozen.

Produced in 1964, this recipe booklet aimed to help with every aspect of preparing for a party, including menu planning and recipes to cook in advance.

ENTERTAINING
WITH STORK

Chocolate and Salted Caramel Fondants

These show-stopping puddings ooze deliciousness when eaten. They can be prepared in advance and baked just before serving.

MAKES 6

150g (5oz) Stork® block, cubed, plus extra for brushing

25g (1oz) cocoa powder, sifted, for dusting

150g (5oz) dark chocolate (70% cocoa solids), broken into pieces

3 large eggs

120g (4½oz) caster sugar

75g (3oz) plain flour

FOR THE SALTED CARAMEL FILLING

50g (2oz) light muscovado sugar

100ml (3½fl oz) double cream

1 tsp vanilla extract

Pinch of sea salt

1. Brush six 200ml (7fl oz) ramekins or 8 individual pudding basins with melted Stork® and line the bottom of each one with a circle of non-stick baking paper. Dust with the cocoa powder, tap out the excess and place the dishes in the fridge until required.
2. To make the filling, place all the ingredients for it in a saucepan over a low heat and stir until the sugar has melted. Increase the heat and bring to the boil, then continue heating until the mixture has slightly thickened. Set aside to cool completely.
3. Pour the cold filling into 6 holes in an ice-cube tray and freeze for 2 hours, or until completely set.
4. To make the fondants, melt the cubed Stork® and chocolate in a heatproof bowl set over a pan of simmering water. Set aside to cool slightly.
5. Meanwhile, whisk the eggs and sugar together until the mixture leaves a trail across the surface when the whisk is lifted.
6. Sift half the flour over the egg mixture and fold in with a large metal spoon. Add half the melted chocolate and fold that in too. Continue folding in the remaining flour and chocolate alternately until all used up and the mixture is streak-free.
7. Place the prepared dishes on a baking tray and divide half the batter between them. Place a frozen cube of caramel in each dish, then add the remaining batter, making sure the dishes are no more than three-quarters full. Chill for 2 hours, or freeze.
8. Preheat the oven to 200°C/400°F/Gas Mark 6.
9. Bake the puddings for 11–13 minutes, adding a few more minutes if you're baking them from frozen. A crust should form that is firm around the edge but a little soft in the centre, and the fondants should just be starting to come away from the sides. Leave to stand for 1 minute before turning out. Serve with cream.

Maple Syrup and Walnut Steamed Pudding

On a cold winter's day there's nothing like a hearty steamed pudding served with lashings of custard to cheer everyone up. Comfort food at its best.

SERVES 6–8

175g (6oz) Stork® spread, plus extra for brushing

75g (3oz) pecans or walnuts, roughly chopped

2 tbsp maple syrup

175g (6oz) self-raising flour

1 tsp baking powder

175g (6oz) golden caster sugar

3 large eggs, beaten

2 tbsp milk

FOR THE TOFFEE SAUCE

75g (3oz) Stork® spread

100g (4oz) light muscovado sugar

3 tbsp double cream

1. Generously brush a 1.2 litre (2 pint) pudding basin with melted Stork® and line the bottom with a circle of non-stick baking paper. Cut out a 35cm (14 inch) square of foil and also brush with melted Stork®.
2. Scatter the nuts in the bottom of the pudding basin and add the maple syrup. Set aside.
3. Place the flour and baking powder in a large bowl. Add the Stork®, sugar, eggs and milk and beat with an electric whisk for a few minutes, until smooth.
4. Spoon the batter into the basin and level the surface. Place the foil on a work surface, oiled side up, and fold 2 pleats in the centre. Place this, oiled side down, on top of the basin. Tie with string around the rim, and loop it loosely over the top to create a handle. Trim off any excess foil.
5. Place the pudding basin on a trivet or upturned saucer in a large saucepan and pour in enough boiling water to come two-thirds of the way up the side of the basin. Cover with a lid, bring to a simmer and steam for 2 hours, occasionally topping up with boiling water if necessary.
6. When the pudding is ready, make the sauce by melting the Stork® and sugar together in a small pan. When the sugar has dissolved, stir in the cream and simmer for 1 minute.
7. Meanwhile, loosen the pudding from the bowl by running a table knife around it, then carefully invert it onto a plate. Serve with the sauce drizzled over it.

Stork®'s *Family File* booklets offered not just great recipes, but practical ideas for balancing rest and play.

Family File

Getting the family together

Making the most of your kitchen. Kitchen equipment.
Home made food: day by day. The art of pastry making.
Creative use of your freezer. Ideas for play.

Stork Cookery Service

Caramel Self-saucing Pudding

The perfect Sunday lunch pudding, this has an amazing sauce that magically appears under the spongy top. Yum!

SERVES 6

100g (4oz) Stork® spread, plus extra for brushing

275g (10oz) self-raising flour

1 tsp baking powder

150g (5oz) light muscovado sugar

250ml (8fl oz) milk

3 eggs

FOR THE SAUCE

150g (5oz) light muscovado sugar

4 tbsp golden syrup

300ml (10fl oz) boiling water

1. Preheat the oven to 180°C/350°F/Gas Mark 4. Brush a 28 x 20 x 4cm (11 x 8 x 1½ inch) baking dish with melted Stork®.
2. Place the Stork®, flour, baking powder, sugar, milk and eggs in a large bowl and beat well with a wooden spoon until just smooth. Pour into the prepared dish.
3. Combine all the sauce ingredients in a separate bowl and stir until the sugar has dissolved. Pour the mixture evenly over the batter, then bake for 45–50 minutes, or until the sponge feels just firm in the centre. Serve hot with ice cream.

Marmalade Bread and Butter Pudding

Memories of childhood come rushing back with this pudding. It's a simple dish made even tastier with the citrusy flavour of marmalade.

Serves 6

50g (2oz) Stork® spread, plus extra for brushing

8 slices of bread

3 tbsp Seville orange marmalade

3 eggs

500ml (17fl oz) milk

25g (1oz) caster sugar

1. Preheat the oven to 180°C/350°F/Gas Mark 4. Brush a 1 litre (1¾ pint) ovenproof dish with melted Stork®.
2. Spread each slice of bread with the Stork® and marmalade. Cut the slices in half to make triangles, then arrange them snugly in the prepared dish.
3. Beat the eggs, milk and sugar together in a jug and pour this mixture over the bread. Leave to soak for 10 minutes.
4. Bake for 30 minutes, or until golden brown and the custard has set.

Produced by Stork® in the 1960s, this recipe booklet introduced home cooks to rich bakes and hearty dishes familiar to country dwellers, yet really appealing to everyone.

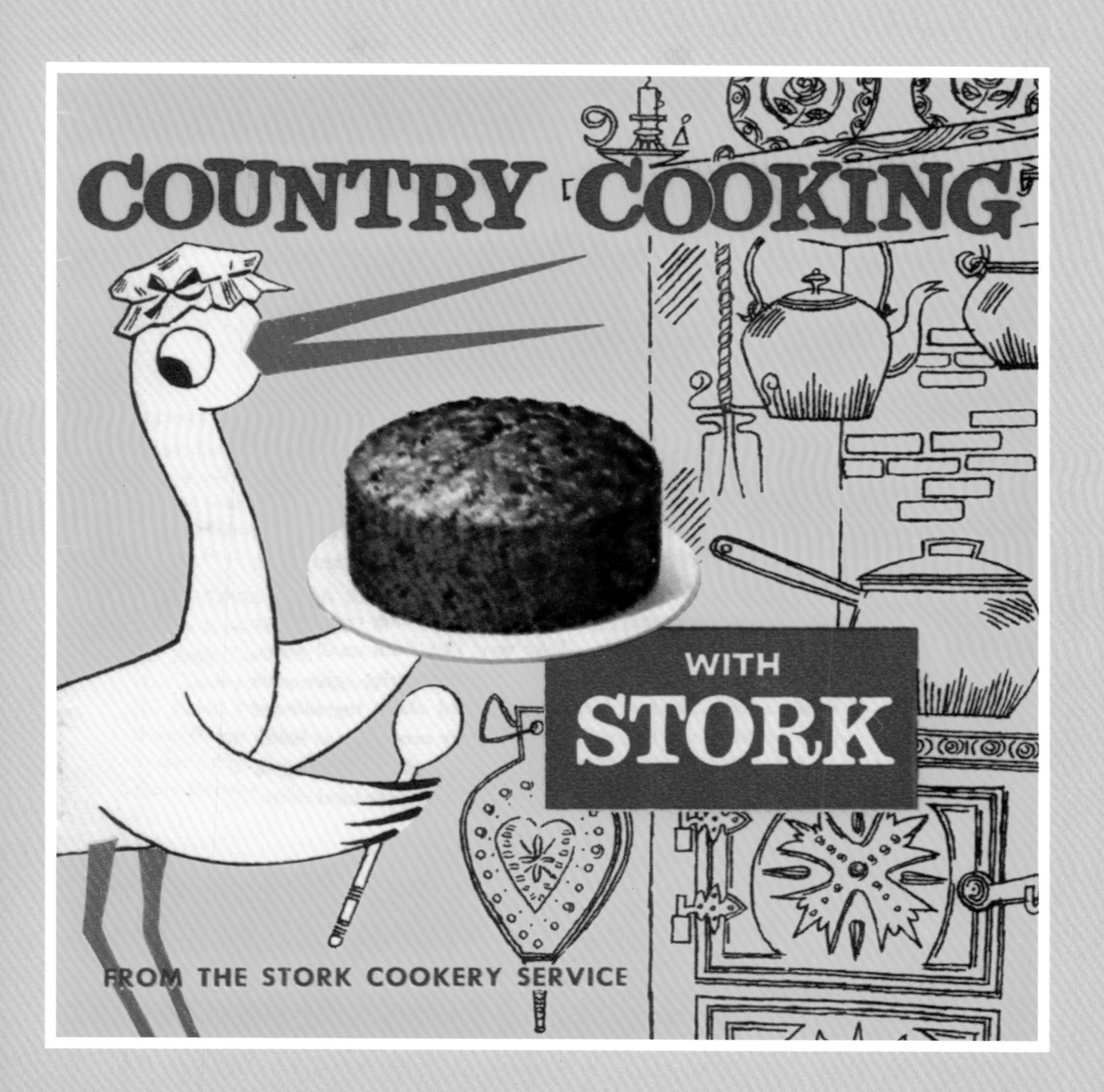
COUNTRY COOKING
WITH
STORK
FROM THE STORK COOKERY SERVICE

Rhubarb and Orange Crumble

Who doesn't love a crumble? The flavour combination here is a classic, but feel free to swap the rhubarb for apples, blackberries or plums, and to add a few chopped nuts to the crumble topping if you like.

SERVES 6

450g (1lb) rhubarb
100g (4oz) caster sugar
Zest and juice of 1 orange
225g (8oz) plain flour
120g (4½oz) Stork® block, cubed
110g (4¼oz) demerara sugar

1. Preheat the oven to 180°C/350°F/Gas Mark 4.
2. Cut the rhubarb into 2.5cm (1 inch) chunks and place them in a 1 litre (1¾ pint) ovenproof dish. Sprinkle with the caster sugar and stir in the orange zest and juice.
3. Place the flour in a bowl and rub in the Stork® until the mixture resembles breadcrumbs. Stir in the demerara sugar.
4. Sprinkle the crumble evenly over the rhubarb and bake for 35–40 minutes, until golden brown and the rhubarb is tender.

Vegan Coconut and Mango Mousse Cake

When mangoes aren't available, top this impressive dessert with your favourite fruits. Strawberries and passion fruit would make a great combination.

SERVES 8

75g (3oz) Stork® block

200g (7oz) dairy-free oat biscuits

1 x 400ml (14fl oz) can coconut milk

8 tsp agar agar flakes

150g (5oz) coconut cream

150ml (5fl oz) dairy-free coconut yoghurt

50ml (2fl oz) maple syrup

Zest and juice 1½ limes

FOR THE TOPPING

1 mango, sliced

Zest of ½ lime

Pulp from 1 passion fruit

1. Line the bottom of a round 20cm (8 inch) loose-bottomed flan or cake tin with non-stick baking paper.
2. Melt the Stork® in a small pan. Meanwhile, place the biscuits in a plastic bag and bash with a rolling pin until they are fine crumbs. Tip the biscuits into the Stork®, mix well, then press into the prepared tin. Leave to set in the fridge for 30 minutes.
3. Place the coconut milk in a small pan, stir in the agar agar and heat gently, without boiling, for 10 minutes, until the flakes have completely dissolved. Set aside to cool for 5 minutes.
4. Put the coconut cream, yoghurt, maple syrup and lime juice into a bowl and whisk together. Stir in the warm coconut milk and set aside for 10 minutes to thicken slightly.
5. Pour the thickened mixture into the flan tin, where it will set quite quickly even at room temperature. If not needed straight away, store in the fridge until required.
6. When you're ready to serve, remove the cake from the tin and transfer to a plate. Top with the sliced mango, lime zest and passion fruit.

Vegan Chocolate Tartlets

Crumbly sweet pastry cases filled with a rich chocolate cream and topped with tangy fruit make a stylish dinner party dessert.

MAKES 4 X 10CM (4 INCH) TARTLETS

150ml (5fl oz) soya alternative to cream

1 tbsp maple syrup

150g (5oz) dairy-free dark chocolate (50% cocoa solids)

25g (1oz) Stork® block

200g (7oz) blueberries or raspberries, to decorate

FOR THE PASTRY

100g (4oz) plain flour, plus extra for dusting

Pinch of salt

65g (2½oz) Stork® block, cubed

15g (½oz) caster sugar

3 tsp water

1. Preheat the oven to 200°C/400°F/Gas Mark 6. Set out four 10cm (4 inch) flan tins that are 4cm (1½ inches) deep.
2. To make the pastry, sift the flour and salt together into a bowl. Add the Stork® and rub in until the mixture resembles fine breadcrumbs. Stir in the sugar, then add the water and mix with knife to create a firm dough. Using your hands, shape it into a ball.
3. Cut the dough into 4 equal pieces and roll each into a circle about 19cm (7½ inches) wide.
4. Ease the pastry into each tin and trim off the excess with a knife. Line with a circle of non-stick baking paper, fill with baking beans and bake for 15 minutes, until golden. Remove the paper and beans and return the pastry cases to the oven for a further 5 minutes. Set aside to cool.
5. Place the cream alternative and maple syrup in a pan and bring to the boil. Remove from the heat and add the chocolate, stirring until melted.
6. Add the Stork® and stir until smooth. Allow to cool at little, then pour the chocolate mixture into the pastry cases and leave to set in the fridge.
7. When cold, top with the berries.

Note: These tartlets will keep in the fridge for up to 3 days.

Stork® has an unrivalled reputation for making great bakes, but as this 1960s advertisement makes clear, its creaminess and flavour have always made it a very popular alternative to butter.

HERE IT IS . . .
NEW
STORK
- new creamier taste!
NEW STORK
New Creamier Taste

Vegan Banoffee Pie

Rich coconut cream and almond milk make a delicious custard to pour over the yummy topping of date purée and sliced banana on this tasty biscuit base.

SERVES 8

200g dairy-free oat biscuits

100g (4oz) Stork® block, melted

200ml (7fl oz) unsweetened almond milk

4 tbsp cornflour

2 tbsp light muscovado sugar

250ml (8fl oz) coconut cream

175g (6oz) dried dates

50ml hot water

3 bananas

50g (2oz) dark dairy-free chocolate

1. Set out a 20cm (8 inch) flan tin.
2. Place the biscuits in a plastic bag and bash with a rolling pin until they are fine crumbs. Tip into a bowl, add the melted Stork® and mix well.
3. Press the biscuit mixture into the flan tin, pressing it firmly up the sides. Leave to set in the fridge for 20 minutes.
4. Spoon 6 tablespoons of the almond milk into a small bowl and add the cornflour and sugar.
5. Place the remaining almond milk and the coconut cream in a small pan and heat to just below boiling point. Stir in the cornflour mixture and cook, stirring constantly, until thickened and smooth. Leave to cool for 15 minutes.
6. Place the dates and water in a small pan, bring to a simmer, then mash to a purée. Spread over the biscuit base.
7. Slice one banana and arrange over the date mixture, then pour over the cooled custard. Leave to set in the fridge for 2 hours.
8. Just before serving, slice the remaining bananas and arrange on top of the custard.
9. Melt the chocolate in heatproof bowl set over a pan of simmering water, then drizzle it over the bananas. Serve the pie in slices.

is always ready to help you.
If you have any cookery queries
or require any recipes,
do get in touch with us.

Pumpkin Toffee Crispies

Seriously sticky, seriously cute and seriously yummy ... it will be hard to resist these adorable little pumpkins at Halloween.

MAKES 16–18

120g (4½oz) Stork® block

120g (4½oz) creamy toffees, or fudge, broken into pieces

120g (4½oz) marshmallows

120g (4½oz) puffed rice

1 tsp orange gel colouring

FOR THE DECORATION

16–18 chocolate fingers, cut in half

Green fondant icing

1. Line a baking sheet with non-stick baking paper.
2. Place the Stork®, toffees and marshmallows in a large pan and stir over a very gentle heat until melted and blended together.
3. Take the pan off the heat and stir in the puffed rice and food colouring.
4. Using a tablespoon, place 16–18 mounds of the mixture on the prepared baking sheet. Insert half a chocolate finger into each one and allow to set for about 5 minutes.
5. Once slightly less sticky, form the mounds into pumpkin-shaped balls.
6. Roll out the icing, cut out 16–18 small leaf shapes and place them beside the chocolate 'stems'.

There is always a reason to celebrate, so Stork® produced this book of 'exciting savouries and tempting cakes and cookies' to make every party go with a swing.

PARTY
TIME
with
Stork

Stork® Christmas Cake

Here we have the perfect fruit cake. It's traditional to make this on Stir-up-Sunday, about five weeks before Christmas, and feed it with spoonfuls of brandy, but it's a great cake even when made a day or two before.

SERVES 20

450g (1lb) raisins
375g (13oz) currants
375g (13oz) sultanas
150g (5oz) cherries washed dried and halved
150g (5oz) glacé fruit or mixed cut peel
100g (4oz) chopped almonds
Grated zest of 2 lemons
Grated zest of 1 orange
6 tbsp whisky, brandy or rum
350g (12oz) Stork® spread
350g (12oz) dark brown sugar
425g (15oz) plain flour
1 tsp ground mixed spice
½ tsp ground nutmeg
75g (3oz) ground almonds
7 large eggs

FOR THE DECORATION

1 tbsp apricot jam
Icing sugar, for dusting
250g (9oz) marzipan
500g (1lb 2oz) ready-to-roll icing
Edible glue (from cake decorating shops)
Edible silver balls
Sprig of holly

1. Preheat the oven to 140°C/275°F/Gas Mark 1. Brush a 25cm (10 inch) round cake tin or a 23cm (9 inch) square cake tin with melted Stork® and fully line with a double thickness of non-stick baking paper. (If your oven tends to run hot, tie a single thickness of brown paper around the outside of the tin.)
2. Place all the fruit, almonds and zests in a bowl. Pour in the alcohol, mix well, then cover and leave overnight.
3. The next day, place all the remaining ingredients in a very large bowl, add the soaked fruit and beat until thoroughly mixed (3–4 minutes).
4. Place this mixture in the prepared tin, smooth the top with the back of a wet tablespoon and bake for 5–6 hours. Check at intervals after 3 hours as ovens tend to vary. Cover the cake with doubled non-stick baking paper or foil for about the last 1–2 hours to prevent the top becoming too brown.
5. When the centre top of the cake feels firm when pressed with your fingers, insert a clean, warm skewer and if it comes out clean, the cake is ready. At this stage there should be no sizzling noise coming from the cake. Set aside to cool in the tin overnight, then turn out and peel off the paper. Store as described on page 211.
6. To decorate, brush the top of the cake with the apricot jam. Dust a work surface with icing sugar and roll the marzipan into a circle that sits neatly on top of the cake.
7. Roll the icing into a circle about 12cm (5 inches) larger than the cake. Using a knife, cut around the edge to create a wavy line. Drape the icing over the cake and press it onto the marzipan.
8. Using a paintbrush, dot the edible glue at regular intervals around the top of the cake, then press a silver ball onto each dot. Arrange the holly and more silver balls in the centre.

Note: The cake will keep for up to 2 months in an airtight container.

SO CREAMY!”

Hot Cross Buns

Easter is a time for home baking, and freshly baked hot cross buns are a real treat. Why not get the family involved in making them too?

MAKES 8

25g (1oz) Stork® spread, plus extra for brushing

225g (8oz) strong plain flour, plus extra for dusting

1 tsp salt

1 x 7g sachet easy-blend yeast

40g (1½oz) caster sugar

50g (2oz) mixed dried fruit

25g (1oz) mixed chopped peel

1 tsp ground mixed spice

150ml (5fl oz) semi-skimmed milk

Vegetable oil, for greasing

FOR THE CROSSES

50g (2oz) plain flour

25g (1oz) Stork® block

4 tbsp water

FOR THE GLAZE

2 tbsp sugar

1 tbsp milk

1. Preheat the oven to 220°C/425°F/Gas Mark 7. Brush a baking sheet with melted Stork®.
2. Put the Stork® into a large bowl, sift in the flour and salt, then rub together until the mixture resembles fine breadcrumbs.
3. Stir in the yeast, sugar, fruit, peel and mixed spice.
4. Warm the milk until tepid, pour it into the bowl and mix well to form a soft dough.
5. Place the dough on a floured work surface and knead until elastic and no longer sticky. Shape into 8 buns and place them on the prepared baking sheet. Cover with lightly oiled clingfilm and leave in a warm place for about 45 minutes, until almost doubled in size.
6. To make the cross mixture, put the flour into a bowl and rub in the Stork®, then stir in the water. Spoon into a piping bag fitted with a large nozzle.
7. Uncover the risen buns and pipe the cross mixture onto them.
8. Bake for 15 minutes, or until golden brown and cooked through.
9. To make the glaze, gently warm the sugar and milk together. Brush the glaze over the buns, then pop them back into the oven for another 2 minutes. Transfer to a plate or wire rack to cool before serving.

As the introduction to this 1950s booklet says, the Stork® Cookery Service provided recipes that would 'fit the bill' for every occasion, from coffee mornings to special celebrations.

CAKES
FOR ALL OCCASIONS
STORK
COOKERY SERVICE

Simnel Buns

These marzipan buns not only taste great, but make a wonderful centrepiece for your Easter table. You could even add a little grated dark chocolate to the filling if you want to get every Easter flavour in one bake.

MAKES 12

500g (1lb 2oz) strong white flour, plus extra for dusting

1 tsp salt

2 tsp caster sugar

1 x 7g sachet easy-blend yeast

150ml (5fl oz) tepid water

120ml (4fl oz) milk

1 large egg

40g (1½oz) Stork® block

Vegetable oil, for greasing

FOR THE FILLING

75g (3oz) Stork® block

75g (3oz) dark brown muscovado sugar

1 tsp ground mixed spice

75g (3oz) marzipan, cut into small chunks

100g (4oz) dried mixed fruit

50g (2oz) almonds, roughly chopped

FOR THE GLAZE

4 tbsp apricot jam

1 tbsp water

1. Place the flour in a bowl and stir in the salt and sugar. Stir in the yeast, then add the water, milk and egg and mix well with a wooden spoon or your hands until you have a scraggy dough. Work in the Stork®, then knead for 10 minutes by hand, or 5 minutes in an electric mixer fitted with a dough hook, until the mixture is smooth and elastic.
2. Place the dough in an oiled bowl, cover with oiled clingfilm and allow to rise until doubled in size – usually an hour, but could be more if your kitchen is cool.
3. Meanwhile, start making the filling by creaming together the Stork®, sugar and mixed spice until paste-like.
4. Once the dough has risen, flour a work surface and roll the dough into a 45cm (18 inch) square. Spread the filling paste all over the dough, then sprinkle with the marzipan, fruit and nuts. Roll up tightly, trim off the messy ends and cut the roll into 12 equal slices (see Note below). Place these, spiral side up, in a roasting tray and allow to rise for another 30 minutes.
5. To make the glaze, simply boil together the apricot jam and water for 1 minute.
6. Preheat the oven to 220°C/425°F/Gas Mark 7.
7. Bake the buns for 15 minutes, or until risen and golden. As soon as they come out of the oven, brush them with the apricot glaze and allow to cool in the tin.

Note: To slice the roll without damaging the shape of the pieces, take a length of unflavoured dental floss and slide it underneath the roll where you want to make the first cut. Cross it over the top and pull it tight to slice. Repeat to make the required number of slices.

White Chocolate Lamb Cake

As you can see, this is such a cute cake that it's almost too good to cut. However, the white chocolate sponge and icing is too good to miss, so get that knife out!

SERVES 12

150g (5oz) Stork® spread, plus extra for brushing

200g (7oz) caster sugar

2 eggs

200g (7oz) plain flour

¾ tsp bicarbonate of soda

¼ tsp baking powder

120g (4½oz) white chocolate, melted

170ml (scant 6fl oz) buttermilk

½ tsp vanilla extract

FOR THE FROSTING

100g (4oz) white chocolate, melted

200g (7oz) Stork® spread

250g (9oz) icing sugar

FOR THE DECORATION

Chocolate writing tube

Ready-to-roll icing, pink and white

1. Preheat the oven to 180°C/350°F/Gas Mark 4. Brush two 20cm (8 inch) cake tins with melted Stork® and line the bottom with non-stick baking paper.
2. Cream the Stork® and sugar until light, then gradually beat in the eggs.
3. Sift the flour, bicarbonate of soda and baking powder into the mixture, add the chocolate, buttermilk and vanilla and stir until well blended.
4. Divide the mixture between the prepared tins and bake for 25–30 minutes, until golden and springy to the touch. Turn onto a wire rack to cool.
5. To make the frosting, place all the ingredients for it in a bowl and beat together until smooth. Place half the frosting in a piping bag fitted with a large star nozzle.
6. Sandwich the cakes together with 2 tablespoons of the frosting left in the bowl, then spread a thin layer of it over the surface of the cake with a palette knife.
7. Pipe swirls of frosting around the perimeter and sides of the cake.
8. Use the chocolate writing tub to pipe the eyes and mouth, as shown in the photo.
9. Roll out the pink and white icings and cut out the ears and nose. Position them on the cake, as shown opposite.

Gluten-free Easter Cupcakes

Make sure everyone gets to enjoy Easter treats with these cupcakes, which take just a few minutes to make.

Gf

MAKES 12

100g (4oz) gluten-free self-raising flour

1 tbsp cocoa powder

½ tsp gluten-free baking powder

100g (4oz) Stork® block, cubed

100g (4oz) caster sugar

2 large eggs

2 tbsp milk

Mini chocolate Easter eggs

FOR THE CHOCOLATE ICING

75g (3oz) Stork® spread

1–2 tbsp milk

1 rounded tbsp cocoa powder

225g (8oz) icing sugar, less 1 tbsp, sifted

1. Preheat the oven to 190°C/375°F/Gas Mark 5. Line a 12-hole cupcake tin with paper cases.
2. Sift the flour, cocoa and baking powder into a bowl. Add the Stork®, sugar, eggs and milk and beat together until well mixed (2–3 minutes).
3. Place rounded teaspoons of the mixture in the paper cases and bake for 15–20 minutes. Cool on a wire rack.
4. To make the icing, place all the ingredients in a bowl and beat until smooth. Spoon into a piping bag fitted with a star nozzle.
5. When the cupcakes are cold, pipe the icing around the top of them to create a nest effect.
6. Pop a few mini Easter eggs into each nest.

Appendix

How to Line a Deep Cake Tin

1. Always start by brushing the inside of the tin with melted Stork®.
2. Sit the tin on a double sheet of non-stick baking paper, mark around it, then cut out the marked circle.
3. For the sides, cut a doubled strip of non-stick baking paper about 5cm (2 inches) higher than the depth of the tin, and long enough to go right around the sides with an overlap of about 2.5cm (1 inch).
4. Along one edge of the doubled strip, turn up a margin about 2.5cm (1 inch) deep. Straighten out and 'snick' with scissors in a sloping direction all along the margin.
5. Put the long strip inside the tin with the snicked margin lying flat all around the bottom. The ends should overlap so that the sides of the tin are completely covered. The lining should stand about 2.5cm (1 inch) above the rim of the tin.
6. Put the circle of baking paper in the bottom of the tin, over the snicked margin.

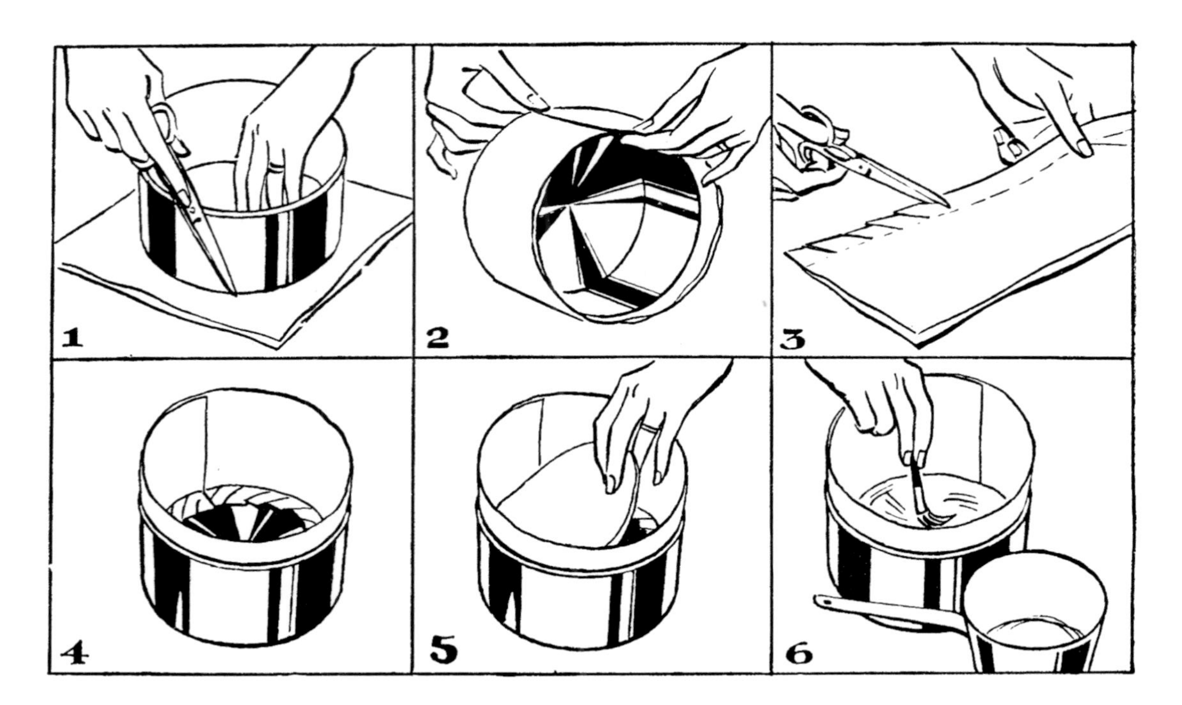

How to Line a Shallow Cake Tin

Unless a recipe states otherwise, shallow tins should be brushed with melted Stork® and lined with just a circle of non-stick baking paper in the bottom.

How to Protect a Fruit Cake While Baking

As rich fruit cakes take a long time to bake, it is advisable to wrap a double thickness of brown paper or newspaper around the outside of the tin and tie it in place with string. The temperature at which fruit cakes are baked is low, so there is little risk of them overbrowning. However, cover with non-stick baking paper if you see signs of this.

How to Store Rich Fruit Cakes

Ensure the cake is completely cold by setting it aside for 24 hours after baking or icing. Whether your cake is iced or not, wrap it in greaseproof or baking paper and store it in an airtight container to keep it moist.

How to Make and Use a Piping Bag

Homemade piping bags can be made from greaseproof paper. While you can snip off the tip and simply start piping, it's worth buying a few nozzles for special designs. Make sure you fit them firmly into the point of the bag.

1. Cut a 30cm (12 inch) square of greaseproof paper.
2. Fold in half to form a triangle and mark the corners A, B and C as shown opposite. Fold point C over to B, then press along the centre from the base to point A; open the triangle out again so that you can see the crease for guidance.
3. Fold corner C up to corner A.
4. Fold corner B right over, flush with the crease down the centre.
5. Pick up the paper with your non-dominant hand, place the fingers of the other hand down opening and fold over corner B until it meets the back of corner A. Corner C is in front. The diagram shows the three corners almost meeting.
6. Fold over the three corners.
7. Tear four slits at the top of the bag and press the resulting flaps down to keep the bag firm. Cut off the point of the bag to give the size of hole required – small for fine piping, or larger if you're going to insert a nozzle (make sure it's pressed firmly into the end opening).
8. Half-fill the bag with icing. Press the top of the bag together, then fold over. Roll the flattened part downwards until the bottom of the bag is tight with icing. To write or pipe borders, press the icing down using both thumbs while keeping a grip on the rolled top, otherwise the heat of the hands will melt the icing.

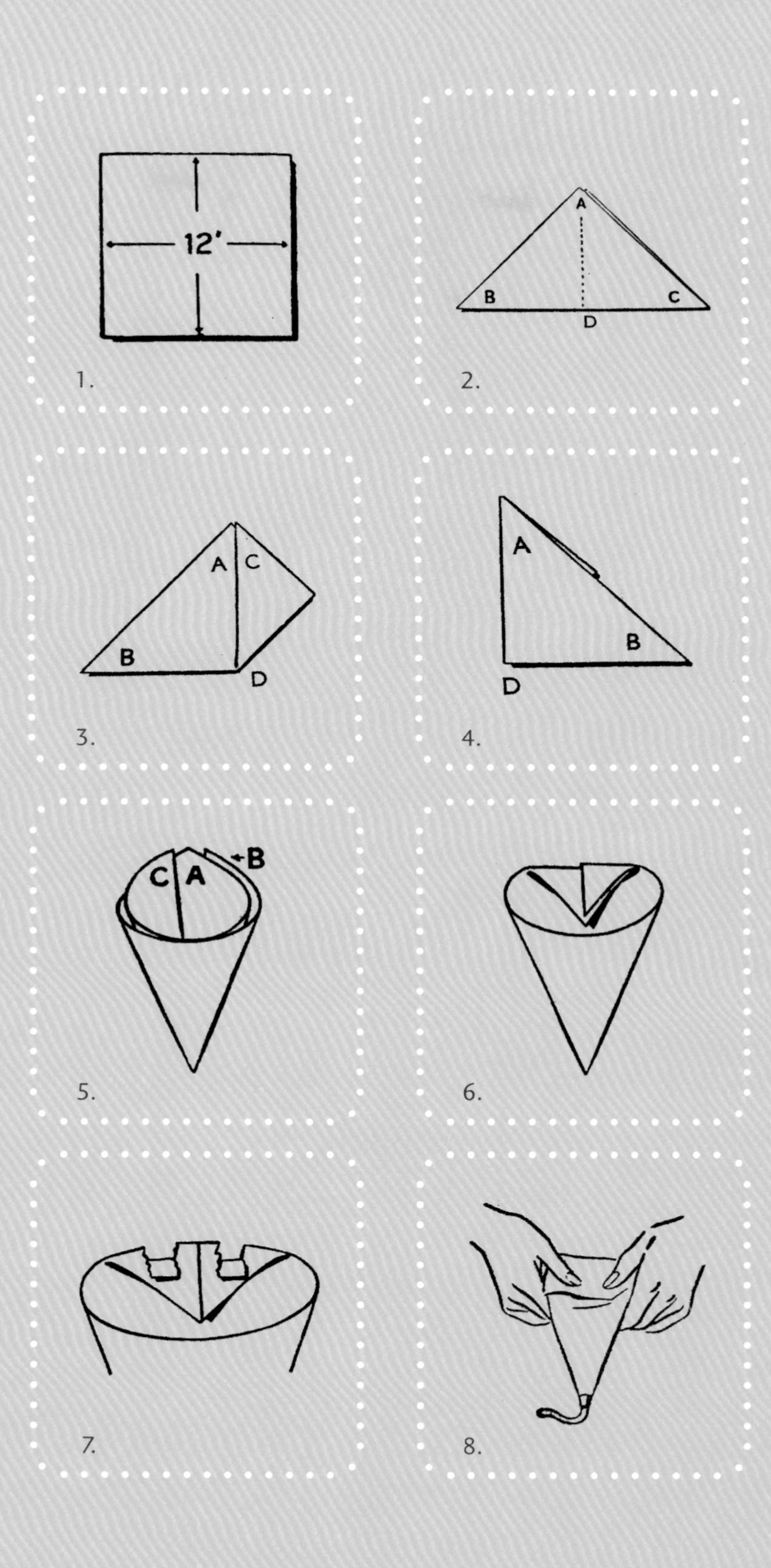
12'
1.
A
B
C
D
2.
A
C
B
D
3.
A
B
D
4.
C
A
B
5.
6.
7.
8.

Ingredient Proportions for Rich Fruit Cakes

TIN SIZE	12cm (5 inch) round	15cm (6 inch) round	18cm (7 inch) round	20cm (8 inch) round	23cm (9 inch) round	25cm (10 inch) round	28cm (11 inch) round	30cm (12 inch) round	33cm (13 inch) round
	10cm (4 inch) square	12cm (5 inch) square	15cm (6 inch) square	18cm (7 inch) square	20cm (8 inch) square	23cm (9 inch) square	25cm (10 inch) square	28cm (11 inch) square	30cm (12 inch) square
INGREDIENT									
Almonds, ground	25g (1oz)	40g (1½oz)	50g (2oz)	65g (2½oz)	75g (3oz)	90g (3½oz)	120g (4½oz)	135g (4¾oz)	150g (5oz)
Almonds, whole	25g (1oz)	40g (1½oz)	65g (2½oz)	90g (3½oz)	120g (4½oz)	150g (5oz)	175g (6oz)	200g (7oz)	225g (8oz)
Black treacle	½ tbsp	1 tbsp	1 tbsp	1 tbsp	1½ tbsp	2 tbsp	2 tbsp	2 tbsp	2½ tbsp
Brandy	1 tbsp	1½ tbsp	2 tbsp	2½ tbsp	3 tbsp	3½ tbsp	4 tbsp	4½ tbsp	5 tbsp
Currants	150g (5oz)	200g (7oz)	275g (10oz)	375g (13oz)	450g (1lb)	550g (1lb 4oz)	675g (1lb 8oz)	800g (1lb 12oz)	900g (2lb)
Eggs	2	3	4	5	6	7	8	9	10
Flour, plain	120g (4½oz)	150g (5oz)	200g (7oz)	250g (9oz)	300g (11oz)	400g (14oz)	450g (1lb)	525g (1lb 3oz)	625g (1lb 6oz)
Glacé cherries	25g (1oz)	40g (1½oz)	65g (2½oz)	90g (3½oz)	120g (4½oz)	150g (5oz)	175g (6oz)	200g (7oz)	225g (8oz)
Lemon zest, grated	½	½	1	1	2	2	2	3	3

TIN SIZE	12cm (5 inch) round	15cm (6 inch) round	18cm (7 inch) round	20cm (8 inch) round	23cm (9 inch) round	25cm (10 inch) round	28cm (11 inch) round	30cm (12 inch) round	33cm (13 inch) round
	10cm (4 inch) square	12cm (5 inch) square	15cm (6 inch) square	18cm (7 inch) square	20cm (8 inch) square	23cm (9 inch) square	25cm (10 inch) square	28cm (11 inch) square	30cm (12 inch) square
INGREDIENT									
Mixed cut peel	25g (1oz)	40g (1½oz)	65g (2½oz)	65g (2½oz)	90g (3½oz)	120g (4½oz)	150g (5oz)	175g (6oz)	200g (7oz)
Mixed spice	¼ tsp	½ tsp	1 tsp	1¼ tsp	1½ tsp	1½ tsp	2 tsp	2½ tsp	3 tsp
Nutmeg	⅛ tsp	¼ tsp	½ tsp	½ tsp	¾ tsp	¾ tsp	1 tsp	1½ tsp	2 tsp
Raisins	50g (2oz)	65g (2½oz)	120g (4½oz)	150g (5oz)	175g (6oz)	200g (7oz)	225g (8oz)	250g (9oz)	275g (10oz)
Soft brown sugar	90g (3½oz)	135g (4¾oz)	175g (6oz)	225g (8oz)	275g (10oz)	350g (12oz)	400g (14oz)	450g (1lb)	500g (1lb 2oz)
Stork®	75g (3oz)	120g (4½oz)	150g (5oz)	200g (7oz)	250g (9oz)	300g (11oz)	375g (13oz)	425g (15oz)	500g (1lb 2oz)
Soft brown sugar	90g (3½oz)	135g (4¾oz)	175g (6oz)	225g (8oz)	275g (10oz)	350g (12oz)	400g (14oz)	450g (1lb)	500g (1lb 2oz)
Sultanas	75g (3oz)	120g (4½oz)	200g (7oz)	250g (9oz)	300g (11oz)	375g (13oz)	450g (1lb)	525g (1lb 3oz)	625g (1lb 6oz)

Troubleshooting Fruit Cake Problems

Most faults arise from using an unbalanced recipe, i.e. the incorrect amounts of Stork®, sugar, egg, fruit, liquid and raising agent in proportion to the flour for the type of cake being made. Very rarely is a cake a failure because of just one fault mentioned below; generally, the failure is due to a combination of faults.

FAULT	CAUSE
Too dry	• Not enough liquid, Stork® or sugar. • Baked too long. • Too much raising agent.
Hard crust outside with damp and doughy centre	• Heat too high, and cake baked too quickly. • Too much liquid, especially in gingerbread types, when syrup is used.
Burnt outside	• Heat too high. • Oven too small for the size of cake. • Tin needed protection a double thickness of brown paper around the outside. • Baked on too high a shelf.
Sunk in middle	• Too much raising agent. • Heat too high. • Oven door opened too soon. • Not baked long enough.
Texture has pronounced holes	• Too much raising agent.
Cracks across the top	• Tin too small. • Heat too high. • Too much raising agent. • Insufficient liquid.
Fruit has sunk to the bottom	• Too much liquid or raising agent. • Too much heavy fruit, e.g. whole cherries. • Fruit not properly washed and dried. • Insufficient creaming.
Texture too close and cake insufficiently risen	• Not enough raising agent or liquid. • Heat too low. • Curdling of mixture when creaming. • Insufficient creaming.
Crumbly texture	• Not enough egg to bind the ingredients. • Too much raising agent. • Baked too long.

Variations on Victoria Sandwich Cake

	ALL-IN-ONE MIXTURE	CREAMED MIXTURE
Chocolate sponge	• 2 tbsp cocoa blended with 2 tbsp hot water, then cooled	• At step 2, add 2 tbsp cocoa blended with 2 tbsp hot water, then cooled, before adding eggs.
Fill the cake and ice the top and sides with Chocolate Icing (see page 157). Roll the sides in chocolate vermicelli. Decorate the top with a piped lattice design and mimosa balls, if liked.		
Coffee and walnut sponge	• 2 tsp instant coffee dissolved in 1 tbsp cooled boiled water • 50g (2oz) chopped walnuts	• At step 2, add 2 tsp cocoa blended with 2 tbsp hot water, then cooled, before adding eggs. • At step 4, fold in 50g (2oz) chopped walnuts with the flour.
Fill and ice with Stork® Coffee Icing (see page 154). Decorate the top with walnut halves.		
Coffee almond ring	• 2 tsp instant coffee dissolved in 1 tbsp boiling water, then cooled • 25g (1oz) ground almonds	• At step 2, add 2 tsp instant coffee dissolved in 1 tbsp boiling water, then cooled, before adding the eggs. • At step 4, fold in 25g (1oz) chopped walnuts with the flour. • At step 4, fold in 50g (2oz) ground almonds with the flour.
Bake in a greased and floured 23cm (9 inch) ring mould. Cover with Coffee Fudge Icing (see page 160). Decorate with melted chocolate.		
Orange or lemon sponge	• Grated zest of an orange or lemon	• At step 2, add the grated zest of an orange or lemon before adding the eggs.
Fill and decorate with Orange or Lemon Stork® Icing (see page 54).		
Toffee walnut sponge	• 25g (1oz) finely chopped walnuts	• At step 2, fold in 50g (2oz) finely chopped walnuts with the flour.
Bake in 15cm (6 inch) sandwich tins brushed with melted Stork® and bottom-lined with non-stick baking paper. Fill and cover with Fudge Icing (see page 160).		
Individual sponges	• 25g (1oz) self-raising flour (making 150g/5oz flour in total)	• At step 2, fold in 150g (5oz) self-raising flour.
Bake in bun tins, brushed with melted Stork® or lined with paper cases, at 190°C/375°F/Gas Mark 5 for 15–20 minutes, or bake in a Swiss roll tin, brushed with melted Stork® and fully lined with non-stick baking paper, at 180°C/350°F/Gas Mark 4 for 20–25 minutes; turn onto a wire rack, peel off the paper and cool; cut into 20 small squares. Decorate with raspberry jam, desiccated coconut and glacé cherries or an icing of your choice (see pages 153– 161).		

Troubleshooting Sponge Cake Problems

FAULT	CAUSE
Sponge Cakes	
Domed top	• Too little raising agent.
Hollowed top	• Too much raising agent.
Close, rather doughy texture, or damp streak at base	• Too much liquid. • Too little flour. • Too much raising agent. • Too much sugar. • Insufficient creaming (of sandwich cakes).
Overbaked outside with soft, doughy centre	• Heat too high. • Baked on too high a shelf.
Baked through but pale	• Heat too low. • Baked on too low a shelf.
Overflowed tin	• Tin too small.
Spots within	• Insufficiently beaten. • Sugar still undissolved before baking.
Stuck to sides of tin, and sticky and damp when cold	• Slightly underbaked; needs 3–5 minutes more.
Too shallow and not risen	• Insufficiently whisked. • Heat too low. • Insufficient raising agent.
Wrinkled on top	• Slightly underbaked. • Tin too small.
Swiss Rolls	
Very crisp edges and dark, overbaked appearance	• Heat too high. • Baked too long.

Pale and flabby	• Heat too low. • Baked on too low a shelf. • Not baked long enough.
Wet and sticky when turned out	• Too much sugar. • Too much liquid. • Insufficient flour. • Insufficiently whisked to dissolve the sugar. • Seriously underbaked.
Thin and badly risen	• Insufficiently whisked to aerate the batter. • Insufficient raising agent.
Unevenly risen	• Batter not spread evenly in the tin.
Cracks when rolled up	• Over- or underbaked. • Baked in too large a tin. • Batter not spread evenly enough in tin. • Ingredients wrongly balanced. • Not rolled quickly enough before cooling. • Edges not trimmed off. • Jam filling too cold.

Troubleshooting Problems with Scones

FAULT	CAUSE
Tough and leathery	• Overhandled. • Insufficient milk added.
Pale and doughy	• Undercooked. • Cooked too slowly.
Poor volume	• Insufficient raising agent. • Overhandled. • Heat too low.
Brown marks inside	• Too much bicarbonate of soda, or added without sifting.

Troubleshooting Pastry Problems

FAULT	CAUSE
All Types of Pastry	
Soggy	• No hole for escape of steam from filling. • Too thinly rolled out. • Too much liquid in filling.
Uneven rising	• Uneven pressure in rolling: make sure you always roll forwards, never sideways.
Blister on surface	• Water added too slowly or unevenly.
Short or Sweet Pastry and Biscuit Crust	
Hard and tough	• Stork® not well rubbed into flour. • Too much liquid. • Baked too long. • Not enough Stork®. • Over-handled.
Soft, crumbly; difficult to handle	• Too little water. • Too much Stork®. • Too much raising agent.
Pale on top/Not cooked underneath	• Heat too low. • Placed too low in oven. • Not baked long enough.
Dark on top/Scorched edges	• Heat too high. • Baked too long.
Bottom pastry rising in flans/tarts	• Pastry case not blind baked before filling is added (see page 128, step 3). • Base not pricked before baking.

FAULT	CAUSE
Rough Puff, Flaky and Puff Pastry	
Poor volume and too close	• Stork® too soft. • Dough not rested enough.
Not flaky enough	• Too heavily rolled out, or too much rolling. • Too much raising agent. • Heat too low. • Baked on too low a shelf.
Outside crisp, inside heavy and damp	• Heat too high, baking outside too quickly and keeping steam inside the pastry. • Too much water. • Rolled out too thickly.
Rough and uneven on top	• Dough not kneaded enough. • Badly rolled.
Very oily, with fat running onto baking sheet	• Heat too low. • Stork® too soft and oily or too hard when rolling. • Edges not sealed before rolling. • Rolling too heavy.
Pale in colour	• Not baked long enough. • Heat too low. • Baked on too low a shelf.
Dark and crumbly at edges	• Baked too long. • Heat too high.
Hard	• Too much water. • Heat too low. • Baked too long at too low a temperature.
Pastry shrinking from sides of dish	• Stretched or pulled when placed on dish. • Heat too low.
Pastry soggy inside pie	• Filling not cooled before added to dish, or too liquid. • Hole not made to let steam escape.
Crispness lost too quickly	• Oven too hot. • Insufficiently baked throughout. • Stored in over-damp atmosphere.

Index

A

apple:
- apple and blackberry turnovers 142
- apple pie 137
- toffee apple ring 98
- vegan strawberry apple tart 150

avocado, chocolate and lime cake, vegan and gluten-free 78

B

Bakewell tart 130

banana:
- banana loaf 27
- vegan banana, date and apricot bars 102
- vegan banana bread with sticky toffee sauce 48

banoffee pie, vegan 184

Battenberg cake 58

blondies: *see* brownies

blue cheese and sage scones 38

blue monster muffins 41

blueberry and lemon buns, gluten-free 42

Bourbon biscuits 116

bread:
- basic white bread 16
- cheesy walnut rolls 20
- cranberry and mixed seed bloomer 24
- fruity Irish soda bread 26
- garlic and herb tear-and-share bread 22
- gluten-free white bread 44
- traditional brown bread 18
- vegan wheaten bread 45

bread and butter pudding, marmalade 176

brownies:
- chocolate brownies 88
- raspberry blondies 86
- white chocolate blondies 84

buns:
- cinnamon and raisin Chelsea buns 28
- gluten-free blueberry and lemon buns 42
- hot cross buns 200
- simnel buns 202

C

cake tins, lining 210, 211

caramel fingers 110

caramel icing 156

caramel self-saucing pudding 174

caraway and lemon loaf cake 70

carrot cake 64

cheese:
- blue cheese and sage scones 38
- cheesy walnut rolls 20
- spinach, red pepper and cheese scones 36

cheesecake, wholemeal lemon 166

Chelsea buns 28

cherry cake 72

chocolate:
- chocolate and salted caramel fondants 170
- chocolate brownies 88
- chocolate chip cookies 108
- chocolate crackle cookies 118
- chocolate crispies 109
- chocolate icing 157
- chocolate swirl cake 56
- gluten-free and vegan avocado, chocolate and lime cake 78
- vegan chocolate fudge cake 80
- vegan chocolate tartlets 182
- *see also* white chocolate

Christmas cake, Stork 194

cinnamon and raisin Chelsea buns 28

coconut:
- gluten-free raspberry and coconut slice 100
- vegan coconut and mango mousse cake 180

coffee:
- coffee walnut cake 67
- Irish coffee cake 54

cranberry:
- cranberry and mixed seed bloomer 24
- vegan oat and cranberry cookies 122

cupcakes:
- gluten-free Easter cupcakes 206
- Halloween spider cupcakes 190
- mango and lime cupcakes 90

custard tart 136

D

doughnuts, baked s'mores 30

E

Easter cupcakes, gluten-free 206

Eccles cakes 94

éclairs 134

F

flapjacks 95

Florentines, vegan 124

fruit cake, rich 74
- ingredient proportions 214–15

protecting while baking 211
storing 211
troubleshooting problems 216

fruity Irish soda bread 26

fudge icing 160

G

garlic and herb tear-and-share bread 22

ginger and marmalade traybake 96

gingerbread, sticky 198

glacé icing 158

gluten-free:
avocado, chocolate and lime cake 78
blueberry and lemon buns 42
Easter cupcakes 206
lime and raspberry jammy dodgers 120
orange polenta cake 76
raspberry and coconut slice 100
vegan banana bread with sticky toffee sauce 48
white bread 44

H

Halloween spider cupcakes 190

honey scones 34

hot cross buns 200

I

Irish coffee cake 54

J

jammy dodgers, gluten-free lime and raspberry 120

K

key lime pie 168

L

lemon:
caraway and lemon loaf cake 70
gluten-free blueberry and lemon buns 42
lemon and elderflower drizzle cake 62
lemon and raspberry scones 35
lemon curd tart 138
lemon meringue pie 128
vegan lemon and almond cake 77
wholemeal lemon cheesecake 166

lime:
gluten-free and vegan avocado, chocolate and lime cake 78
gluten-free lime and raspberry jammy dodgers 120
key lime pie 168
mango and lime cupcakes 90

M

mango:
mango and lime cupcakes 90
vegan coconut and mango mousse cake 180

maple syrup and walnut steamed pudding 172

marmalade bread and butter pudding 176

marshmallow icing 161

meringues 164

mince pies 196

minted pea and bacon quiche 144

muffins:
blue monster muffins 41
classic muffins 40
vegan pecan muffins 46

O

oat and cranberry cookies, vegan 122

orange:
gluten-free orange polenta cake 76
orange cake 66
rhubarb and orange crumble 178

P

pastry, troubleshooting problems 220–1

peanut and raisin cookies 106

pecan muffins, vegan 46

pies:
apple pie 137
key lime pie 168
lemon meringue pie 128
mince pies 196
pork, sweet potato and chorizo pies 146
vegan banoffee pie 184

piping bags, making and using 212–13

plum tart, free-form 140

pork, sweet potato and chorizo pies 146

profiteroles 132

pumpkin toffee crispies 192

Q

quiche, minted pea and bacon 144

R

rainbow piñata cake 188

raspberry:
gluten-free lime and raspberry jammy dodgers 120
gluten-free raspberry and coconut slice 100
lemon and raspberry scones 35
raspberry blondies 86

rhubarb and orange crumble 178

rich small cakes 92

roasted vegetable pizza tart, vegan 148

S

scones:
blue cheese and sage scones 38
honey scones 34
lemon and raspberry scones 35

spinach, red pepper and cheese scones 36
traditional scones 32
troubleshooting problems 219

shortbread fingers 114

simnel buns 202

spinach, red pepper and cheese scones 36

sponge cake, troubleshooting problems 218–19

Stork icing 154

strawberries:
vegan strawberry apple tart 150
white chocolate cake with strawberries 68

Swiss roll 60

T

tarts:
Bakewell tart 130
custard tart 136
free-form plum tart 140
lemon curd tart 138
vegan chocolate tartlets 182
vegan roasted vegetable pizza tart 148
vegan strawberry apple tart 150

toffee apple ring 98

V

vegan:
avocado, chocolate and lime cake 78

banana, date and apricot bars 102
banana bread with sticky toffee sauce 48
banoffee pie 184
chocolate fudge cake 80
chocolate tartlets 182
coconut and mango mousse cake 180
Florentines 124
lemon and almond cake 77
oat and cranberry cookies 122
pecan muffins 46
roasted vegetable pizza tart 148
strawberry apple tart 150
wheaten bread 45

Victoria sandwich cake 52
variations 217

Viennese whirls 112

W

white chocolate:
white chocolate blondies 84
white chocolate cake with strawberries 68
white chocolate lamb cake 204

1 3 5 7 9 10 8 6 4 2

Published in 2020 by Ebury Press, an imprint of Ebury Publishing,
20 Vauxhall Bridge Road
London SW1V 2SA

Ebury Press is part of the Penguin Random House group of companies whose addresses can be found at global.penguinrandomhouse.com

Penguin
Random House
UK

Design: Small Dots

Recipe writing: Mitzie Wilson (pages 22, 24, 35, 36, 38, 42, 44, 45, 46, 70, 76, 77, 78, 80, 84, 90, 96, 100, 102, 112, 116, 118, 120, 122, 124, 140, 142, 144, 146, 148, 150, 168, 170, 172, 174, 176, 178, 180, 182, 184)

Photography: Haarala Hamilton

Food stylists: Mitzie Wilson and Katy McClelland

Prop stylist: Faye Wears

Project editor: Patricia Burgess

First published by Ebury Press in 2020

www.penguin.co.uk

A CIP catalogue record for this book is available from the British Library

ISBN 9781529105513

Printed and bound in China by C&C Offset Printing Co., Ltd

Penguin Random House is committed to a sustainable future for our business, our readers and our planet. This book is made from Forest Stewardship Council® certified paper.